The International Guide to
TROUT FLIES

The International Guide to
TROUT FLIES

BOB CHURCH

STOEGER

First published in Great Britain as
Bob Church's Guide to Trout Flies
by The Crowood Press, Ramsbury, Marlborough, Wiltshire
SN8 2HE, England.

Photography: John Holden

Published by Stoeger Publishing Company,
55 Ruta Court, South Hackensack, New Jersey 07606.

Library of Congress: 87- 060174

ISBN 0-088317-140-6

Distributed to the trade by Stoeger Industries,
55 Ruta Court, South Hackensack, New Jersey 07606.

In Canada, distributed to the trade by
Stoeger Canada Ltd, 169 Idema Road,
Markham, Ontario L3R 1A9.

Manufactured in Great Britain, 1987

This book is dedicated to fly fishermen
throughout the world, for whom
the artificial fly is common currency.

Contents

Foreword

This is the book for which we have all been waiting: Bob Church at his very best. Bob is one of our most accomplished anglers. He is not only well versed in theory, but is a practical fisherman and, unlike many top sportsmen, an excellent teacher. Above all, he radiates enormous enthusiasm.

To appreciate this fully, you must go out with him in a boat on Rutland Water on a very rough day. With anyone else you would yearn to be at home by the fire; with Bob you are persuaded that you are the luckiest man alive to be battling against the elements in an attempt to catch fish! He makes Hemingway's protagonist in *The Old Man and the Sea* seem an unenthusiastic amateur by comparison. With Bob you actually do catch fish; he shows you where they are and how to catch them. It's easy when you know how!

All these qualities – expertise, inventiveness, enthusiasm and teaching skill – make this an excellent book. It tells us not only what fly patterns are available and how to tie them, but also how to use them, making this a valuable book on fishing as well as on flies.

What I like best, perhaps, is that the book deals with both 'ancient and modern' and that every fly is illustrated in full colour. The treatment of traditional flies is a joy. All the favourites are here – Greenwell's, Lunn's, Tup's. The materials from which they are made, fur and feather, are the stuff of magic, of witchcraft. But, after all, fly-tying *is* witchcraft. That applies whether you are making traditional flies from fur and feather or stillwater 'monstrosities' from fluorescent floss,

chenille and Flashabou, and these are also dealt with very well.

Bob, thank goodness, has never succumbed to the snobbery that 'only chalk-stream fishing counts'. For him, to fish fairly, anywhere and by any method, brings pleasure. He has helped considerably in the development of stillwater fishing, pioneering techniques of boat control, of fishing deep water, and devising a number of successful lures. Without stillwaters and the pioneering spirit of Bob Church, Alan Pearson and others, many of us could not have made the transition from coarse to trout fishing. The techniques and lures of stillwater fishing are different from those used on the river, but they have made possible the rapid expansion of trout fishing.

As fly-fishing expands, so does fly-tying. Some anglers tie flies to save money; some for the sheer pleasure of catching a fish on a home-made fly. For yet others, fly-tying has become almost a separate art, bringing tremendous satisfaction from creating a thing of beauty. Some anglers, alas, like myself, have 'too many thumbs' to tie a fly successfully, and, moreover, I have never been able to follow a book's instructions before.

This book is different. It is a book that anyone – including me – can understand. It is real value-for-money and is certain to add further to the great pleasure that so many derive from trout fishing.

John Golding

Acknowledgements

Firstly I must thank John Dennis of The Crowood Press for giving me my head a little in the presentation of this book. After grouping the flies into logical sets, we needed to find the right photographer. Eventually, we settled on John Holden. What a truly professional photographer he is! He solved the problem of achieving a neutral background to the flies and produced pin-sharp transparencies. To him, my thanks.

My thanks go also to my eight guests for their sets of flies: Steve Parton, Stuart Billam, Alan Pearson, Brian Gent, Peter Gathercole, Bob Morey, Sid Knight and Raphael Madriago from Spain. And finally my thanks to my good friend Nick Nicholson, for his excellent poem, which sums up the mood of the book perfectly.

Bob Church

The author with a 5lb wild rainbow trout from Ladybower Reservoir in the Pennines.

On the Trout Waters near Northampton

Master Walton ne'er did cast his fly
On waters that we now hold so dear,
Nor Piscator his worldly questions ply
Concerning reservoirs that lie so near.

Oh, Brother of the Angle, consider now anew
How close lies mighty Rutland, and glorious Grafham, too.
Fortunate you are that here now you reside,
For each one is a challenge; master them with pride.

Adjacent lies little Ravensthorpe, with Eyebrook to the east,
Both magnificent settings on which the eye can feast.
Abundant Draycote to the north, just off the motorway,
A wealth of fish for one to catch on any type of day.
The gem of gems is Pitsford, right outside the door.
Now really, Brother Angler, could we fairly ask for more?

The Master cannot cast his fly
On these waters, oh, so good,
Nor Piscator his questions ply,
But I'm sure they wish they could.

Nick Nicholson

Introduction

As I chatted to an old fly-fisherman one warm summer evening at Pitsford, while we waited for the evening rise, I couldn't help but notice his rod: it was well-kept and made of split-cane. I showed him my latest pride-and-joy, a boron fly-rod, telling him that I was testing another made of Kevlar.

He agreed that the new rods were marvellous and admitted that perhaps he was handicapping himself by persisting with his beloved, but heavy, old wooden rod. I rubbed it in a little, saying: 'It's no good being too old-fashioned; you've missed out on four major changes in rods.' He knew, of course, about fibre-glass and carbon, and he had read an article about boron, but Kevlar was something he had never heard of. I passed him the boron rod for a few casts, and at his second attempt he admitted that this must easily have been the best and longest cast he had ever made. 'All right, you've convinced me', he said. 'I'll be treating myself to a boron rod!'

The conversation then changed to flies. Producing his fly-box, he showed me his collection of beautifully tied flies, nymphs and lures, including some very realistic nymph and bug patterns which were all his original tyings. While I was praising his skills as a fly-tyer, he decided to get his own back on me for being such a know-all. 'One thing is for sure', he said. 'Science and technology may keep on advancing dramatically, but they'll never change the tying of a fly by hand.' I was pleased to agree with him, for there are references to feathered flies being made more than 1,000 years ago. With that, the occasional fish began to rise as the sedges made their appearance on the water. I wished him luck and went off to fish.

I've told this little story because it shows what fly-tying is all about – a personal, rather romantic art carried out entirely by hand. The dressing of artificial flies remains a complete mystery to some fly-fishers, though their numbers are dropping. Yet those who know how to do it, also know that it is really quite easy. Once you have learned how to tie a simple pattern, the rest follows. The technique and principles are virtually the same for all those more difficult-looking patterns.

Let me explain, as briefly as possible, what basic tools a beginner needs and how small a collection of materials will get him started. The tools required are: a good quality, lever-action fly-vice; a spigot bobbin-holder; hackle-pliers; a small pair of sharp scissors; and a dubbing needle.

The list of materials is a little longer: a selection of long-shank and normal-shank fly-hooks; black tying silk; a selection of furs and feathers, such as squirrel tail, pheasant tail feathers, and hen pheasant and mallard wings; two different widths of silver and gold tinsel; silver, gold, copper and lead wire; as many different coloured wools as you can find; a few cards of differently coloured chenille; some peacock herl and ostrich herl; black, white and orange cock capes, with ginger and badger hen; and finally a bottle of black or clear varnish and a chunk of cobbler's wax.

Although the techniques and principles of tying are broadly speaking the same for all patterns, variations do occur in the tying of a lure compared with the tying of a dry fly, or a nymph compared with a wet fly. For that reason, I shall describe one fly of each type in the introductions to each of the sections: lures, wet flies, nymphs, and dry flies. Remember – practice makes perfect. Try each sample several times and note your improvement. Once you get the knack, any of the patterns in this book will be within your grasp. Some of the patterns may show a variation from the original. Where this is so, it is because I feel that the 1980s version is better, and for this I make no apology.

Even though fly-tying by hand will never change greatly, the materials we use to construct our various patterns are changing quite significantly. Some feathers originally specified for a pattern are from birds that are now protected, and we have to use substitutes. These enforced changes have made no difference to the effectiveness of patterns – except perhaps to improve some of them.

Some years ago the importation of jungle cock capes from India was banned because the bird came close to extinction. These much sought-after hackle feathers formed the eyes or cheeks of many salmon flies and quite a few trout wet flies. During summer, a Dunkeld with cheeks of Veniard's substitute jungle cock is still one of the best attractor point-flies for rainbow trout.

Seal's fur dyed in many colours has long formed the bodies of most imitative flies or nymphs, but this wonderfully translucent material will probably soon be unavailable in Britain. Again, there is no need to worry; a number of man-made fibres are equally as good and some, it is said, are even better. I have been using an American bend called Superla dubbing, with which, in a finished fly, you cannot tell the difference. Antron, similar to the American material, is now widely available in Britain and has received enthusiastic reviews.

Several other new materials have come onto the market. Flashabou has become popular in its various shades, but it is the pearl colour which has created the greatest impact with both fly-tyers and trout. Some colours now have 'pearlescent' finishes, and the new phosphorescent Flashabou is, in effect, luminous. There is also a wind-on pearl body material called Bobbydazzlelure, and a Mylar pearl tubing which is useful for slide-on lure bodies. The American midge floss, which is a simple, crinkly, uneven yarn, will, I feel, become very popular. It does away with the need to use dubbing, especially on fine-bodied nymphs.

Hooks, too, have become much more

varied. The new curved Emerger patterns, made by Partridge of Redditch, will, in my opinion, become popular. Alan Pearson tells me he just cannot get enough of the carrot-shaped Draper hooks which he needs for his new range of lures, and I have also found this hook excellent for bottom-crawling larvae patterns. My own favourites from Partridge's range are the Captain Hamilton, heavyweights which I use for all my wet flies and normal small nymphs. The Mustad 9672 long-shank hooks have probably seen the longest service for lures and the larger leaded nymphs.

Many fly-fishing clubs now organise fly-tying evenings during late autumn and winter. The Fly Dressers' Guild has branches throughout Britain and produces a magazine for members. The Guild is well worth joining; membership enables you to watch the experts and talk to them – new ideas are shared for the benefit of all.

Whenever I have a tying session, I always seem to experiment with one thing or another. Last year it was fluorescent materials. These have been around for a few years, and are available in more than simply wool and floss. I have been using fluorescent seal's fur, hackles, marabou, chenille, Glo-brite floss, and even some tying silk. Suffice to say that my results have been much better than they would have been had I not experimented.

One attraction of fly-tying and fly-fishing is that there is always something new to learn. From the moment you catch your first trout on a fly you tied yourself, you too are hooked. You will not be satisfied until your finished flies are neater and more professional than those in the shops. Then, because you are tying such good flies, you will want to make a detailed study of entomology just in case you are missing something. Gradually your catch-rate of trout will increase with your knowledge and experience. The time will come, however, when having caught limit-bag after limit-bag you go out and blank. But this is no bad thing – being brought down to earth is just what is needed to keep you on your toes.

I consider myself very lucky to live in Northampton, for some of the best stillwater trout fishing in Europe is within easy reach. Pitsford, Ravensthorpe, Eyebrook, Grafham, Draycote and Rutland are virtually on my doorstep. I wouldn't move for all the tea in China!

Imitations of the Trout's World, also published by The Crowood Press, which I wrote jointly with Peter Gathercole, will make the perfect companion to this guide. It covers fly-tying techniques in greater detail (you must, for example, learn the whip-finish) and includes a full entomological study of all the aquatic insects, bugs and small fish on which trout feed. It also offers much useful advice on tactics for many of the stillwaters of Great Britain and Ireland. Readers of this book could regularly use *Imitations* as a cross-reference as to when, where and how to use a certain pattern of fly, nymph and lure.

Guest
and Special Selections

Stuart Billam

Stuart is landlord of the Chequers Inn at Stapleford, Nottingham. He is one of the best amateur fly-dressers I know, and some of his original patterns really take some beating. A fine angler, his catches from reservoirs are well known from his articles in *Trout Fisherman*. What isn't so widely known is that he has taken sea trout of 10lb while drifting loch-style in Scotland and many salmon to more than 20lb.

1 Scorpion

COMMENT

This is a hook arrangement rather than a fly, and is a cross between a tube-fly and a tandem lure. It employs a single hook and a treble. (The method of making the mount is described in the introduction to the lure section on page 60.) The easiest way to dress the body is to place the single hook in the vice, tie in the tinsel and oval tinsel at the bend, wind it back towards the treble, and then reverse the direction and continue forwards to the front of the single. The advantage of this type of rig is best seen when trout are nipping the fly from behind.

DRESSING

Rear hook: Size 14 to 10 treble.
Front hook: Size 8 or 6 Partridge SEB 2-Strong Lure.
Tying silk: Black.
Body: Silver tinsel ribbed with oval.
Wing: Insect-green goat's fur with black goat's fur over.
Hackles: Beard hackle of green goat's fur extending to bend of hook. Sparse black cock hackle over.
Cheeks: Jungle cock or substitute.
Head: Black varnish.

2 Stu's Sedge

COMMENT

Sedges are not, as most anglers seem to think, huge flies. I occasionally use a size 10 hook, but only in a big wave. I tie the tails slightly longer than average, as this seems to give the fly a more balanced look. Partridge is an extremely mobile hackle when wet, blending over the wings and a palmered hackle, giving the appearance of a bedraggled, drowned sedge. It is at this stage that sedges are eaten by the trout. A bright emerald-green body seems more successful than olive green.

DRESSING

Hook: Size 12 or 14 Partridge Sproat.
Tying silk: Black.
Tail: A few whisks of red game cock.
Body: Orange, buff, black or green seal's fur according to the colour of the sedge.
Body hackle: Palmered red game cock.
Ribbing: Fine copper wire.
Wings: Mallard or teal wing feathers tied up instead of down as is usual with wet flies.
Hackle: A full collar hackle in front of the wings of two turns of brown partridge hackle.
Head: Black varnish.

1 Scorpion **2** Stu's Sedge **3** Dave's Dibbler **4** Bug-eyed Lure
5 Olive Dun **6** Oakham Orange **7** Hare's-face Nymph **8** Marabou-tailed Muddler

3 Dave's Dibbler

COMMENT

This fly was developed from a pattern devised by Dave Shipman. Dave is a first-class surface fisherman and this fly should be fished right in the surface film when the trout are really high in the water. It can be fished either as a point-fly or as a top dropper. To make the fly fish really high, it sometimes pays to rub it well with a floatant. I prefer to grease the fly rather than the leader; fly wake doesn't deter fish, leader wake does.

DRESSING

Hook: Size 14 to 10 Sproat or Limerick.
Tying silk: Black.
Butt: Silver tinsel ribbed with oval tinsel tied well round the bend.
Body: Black wool or seal's fur.
Ribbing: 3lb Tynex nylon monofilament.
Hackle: Black cock hackle tied palmer fashion and tied down with the nylon ribbing.
Wing: Teal wing feather or a few strands of phosphor-yellow DRF nylon.
Head: Black varnish.

4 Bug-eyed Lure

COMMENT

The eyes can be made from the plastic tops of spray polish cans by means of a hole-puncher. To form the black pupil, make a hole in the centre of the eye and insert a piece of Black Streak. Apply heat to the end of the nylon, thus forming a little bulb. Do the same to the other end of the Black Streak, making a mini barbell. This can then be lashed to the top of the hook-shank with a figure-of-eight tying. Another good version of this fly has white and red eyes. This is a lure for early season and lead-core fishing.

DRESSING

Hook: Size 8, 6 or 4 Wilson low-water salmon double.
Tying silk: Black.
Tail: Generous spray of black marabou.
Body: Black chenille.
Eyes: White plastic or beads painted with black 'pupils'.
Head: Black varnish.

5 Olive Dun

COMMENT

I look upon this as a modern-day version of that old favourite, the Greenwell's Glory. The ribbing of 3lb clear nylon instead of the traditional gold wire gives a startling appearance – a beautiful translucent body with a segmented effect. I also tie a spider version of this fly, for which I build up a slight thorax with dubbed hare's ear and then tie in a sparse collar hackle. This fly is effective both in still and running water when olives are hatching.

DRESSING

Hook: Size 16 to 10 Sproat or Limerick.
Tying silk: Olive.
Tail (optional): Golden-pheasant topping.
Body: Yellow monocord. Many shop-bought patterns have a body tied with olive silk. This makes the fly much too dark when wet.
Ribbing: Ribbed with 3lb clear Tynex monofilament.
Hackle: Two turns of hen Greenwell.
Wing: Mallard or teal feather.
Head: Clear varnish.

6 Oakham Orange

COMMENT

This fly is designed to be fished as a top dropper and to create a disturbance in the water, hence the heavy collar hackle. Sometimes, especially when sun is on the water, a bright fly will fish better than a drab-coloured fly. This is just such a fly. I designed it for Rutland water, but have had great success with it all over England and Scotland. Surprisingly for such a bright, gaudy fly, it is equally acceptable to both brown and rainbow trout. If fish start coming short, change up a size instead of changing down as is usual.

DRESSING

Hook: Size 14 to 10 Sproat or Limerick.
Tying silk: Red.
Tail: Whisks of the brightest hot-orange cock hackle you can find.
Body: Silver tinsel ribbed with oval tinsel.
Hackles: Hot-orange cock. One tied palmer fashion and tied down with the silver ribbing; and two tied in a full collar hackle and pulled slightly back.
Head: Red varnish.

7 Hare's-face Nymph

COMMENT

This fur is much softer than the traditional fur from a hare's ear. It should be picked out until the resultant fly looks a shaggy mass, with the copper ribbing just showing through. The fly takes on a more streamlined shape when it is in the water. It pays to dress a few weighted for varying conditions. It is a good fly for traditional loch-style fishing out of the front of the boat, especially when no fish are showing. Then it seems to bring fish out from nowhere, particularly daphnia-feeders. I have caught more fish on this pattern than on any other.

DRESSING

Hook: Size 8 Partridge Nymph.
Tying silk: Black.
Tail: A few whisks of white cock hackle.
Body: Hair from a hare's face, not ear, which is pale ginger with blue dun at the bottom. Mix well before spinning on to the body.
Ribbing: Four turns of medium copper wire.
Thorax: The same material as the body, but just a slight thickening and not too pronounced, with the top tied down shellback with any speckled feather.
Head: Black varnish.

8 Marabou-tailed Muddler

COMMENT

I like to use this fly late in the season when the trout are fry-feeding. The traditional clipped deer hair head creates a disturbance in the water which is picked up by the mobile marabou tail, creating an enticing wiggle. This fly has a decided advantage over traditional Muddlers in that it can be fished slowly. I always fish it on a floating line. Clip the head so that no more than three inches of 'V' are created in the water.

DRESSING

Hook: Size 8 or 10 Sproat, Captain Hamilton or similar wide-gaped hook.
Tying silk: Black.
Tail: Spray of white marabou at least twice the length of the hook.
Body: Dubbed red seal's fur.
Ribbing: Oval silver tinsel.
Hackle: Dyed red cock hackle tied palmer fashion.
Head: Spun deerhair clipped to shape, leaving a small ruff.

Peter Gathercole

Peter, from Corby, is a professional fly-dresser and a perfectionist. He has tied flies for some of the best anglers. Still only a young man, his interests have turned to photography and entomology, and these days he travels the world with his work.

1 Sedge Pupa

COMMENT

July and August are the months for the sedge pupa. As the sun sets, the pupae of the larger pale sedges begin to rise towards the surface. It is now that fishing the sedge pupa reaches its peak. This particular amber-bodied imitation is a complex pattern, but an effective one. The antennae are optional.

DRESSING

Hook: Size 10 or 12.
Tying silk: Brown.
Body: Angora wool dyed amber.
Rib: Gold wire.
Thorax: Fur dyed brown and dubbed.
Wing-cases: Cinnamon hen tied short.
Hackle: Hare's fur.
Antennae (optional): Bronze mallard.
Head: Fur dyed brown and dubbed. Clear varnish.

2 Hawthorn Fly

COMMENT

Although, where it does occur, its season is limited, the hawthorn fly can be an important insect to the stillwater fly-fisher and a good imitation is called for. This pattern imitates the main recognition points of the natural fly, including the pronounced thorax and those all-important trailing legs. The Hawthorn can be fished wet or dry.

DRESSING

Hook: Size 10 or 12.
Tying silk: Black.
Abdomen: Black feather-fibre.
Rib: Black tying silk.
Thorax: Black feather-fibre.
Wings: Two white hackle-points tied back-to-back.
Legs: Two fibres of swan herl dyed black, each knotted twice.
Hackle: Black hen.
Head: Black varnish.

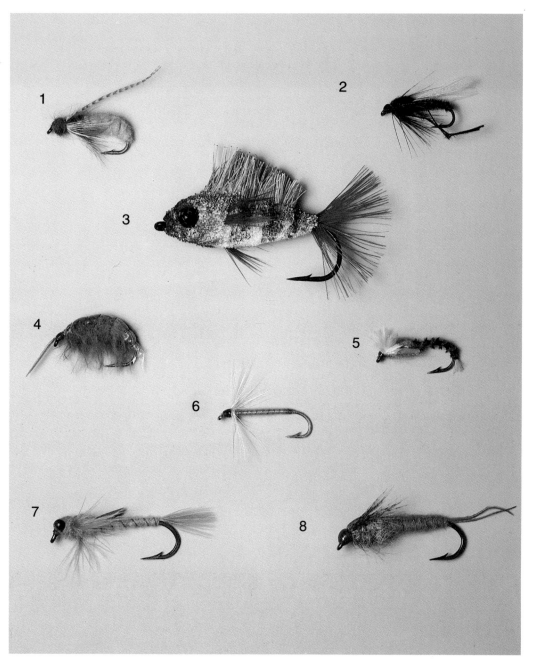

1 Sedge Pupa **2** Hawthorn Fly **3** Deerhair Perch Fry **4** The Shrimp
5 Midge Pupa **6** Phantom Larva **7** Marabou Damsel Nymph **8** Brer Rabbit

3 Deerhair Perch Fry

COMMENT

The Deerhair Perch Fry is most effective at the back-end, when the trout are feeding on the multitude of dead and dying small coarse fish so prevalent at this time of year. The soft deerhair allows the fish to take the lure confidently, ensuring a high proportion of hookable takes.

DRESSING

Hook: Size 2 (two) long-shank.
Tying silk: Black.
Tail: Red cock hackle.
Body: White deerhair spun and clipped to shape and coloured with Pantone pens.
Fins: Red cock hackle-fibres.
Eyes: Metal beads, varnished.

4 The Shrimp

COMMENT

This pattern should be fished on a sink-tip or floating line with a long leader. It can be weighted by binding a few strips of lead foil to the hook-shank before dressing if desired. The weighted version is particularly good for fishing deep or for stalking trout in clear water where the fly must sink to the correct depth as quickly as possible.

DRESSING

Hook: Size 10 or 12 Partridge Grub Hook.
Tying silk: Olive.
Body: Dubbed marabou dyed olive and picked out.
Back: Clear polythene strip.
Rib: Silver wire.
Antennae (optional): Olive feather-fibre.
Head: Clear varnish.

5 Midge Pupa

COMMENT

The pupa of the midge is without doubt the predominant food of the stillwater trout. Many Midge Pupa imitations are available, and this true-to-life pattern can be really effective when fish are proving difficult. The mixed colours of feather-fibre overlaid with polythene strip closely copy the mottling and translucency of the natural pupa during its journey to the surface. Fish take pupae at all depths and tactics must be varied accordingly.

DRESSING

Hook: Size 10, 12 or 14.
Tying silk: Brown.
Tail: White marabou.
Body: Red and black fibres of swan herl.
Rib: Fine polythene strip.
Thorax: Grey rabbit underfur.
Wing-cases: Brown goose biots clipped to shape.
Shell-back: Brown feather-fibre.
Breathing Filaments: White marabou.
Head: Black varnish.

6 Phantom Larva

COMMENT

The imitation of the phantom larva and pupa is only a minor stillwater technique when the trout are taking the naturals. But the fish can become preoccupied with the larvae, and thus a good imitation is needed. The phantom larva, being almost transparent, is not an easy creature to imitate. It is best achieved by using a silvered hook wrapped in clear polythene. Conditions are often calm when phantom larvae and pupae are being taken, and the artificial needs to be fished slowly on a fine leader, with the occasional tweak.

DRESSING

Hook: Size 14 long-shank.
Tying silk: Brown.
Body: Clear polythene strip.
Hackle: White cock tied sparsely.
Head: Clear varnish.

7 Marabou Damsel Nymph

COMMENT

Most Damsel Nymph imitations are dressed too thickly in the body. The use of marabou wound on to the hook-shank ensures that the body remains slim, as in the natural. The feather-fibre creates the necessary movement and life. The damsel nymph emerges from June to late August, according to its species. The artificial Damsel fishes well when moved quite quickly close to the surface.

DRESSING

Hook: Size 8 or 10 long-shank.
Tying silk: Olive.
Tail: Marabou dyed olive.
Body: Marabou dyed olive.
Rib: Copper wire.
Thorax: Marabou dyed olive and dubbed.
Wing-cases: Swan slips dyed olive.
Eyes: 20lb nylon melted into round globules.
Head: Marabou dyed olive.
Head finish: Clear varnish.

8 Brer Rabbit

COMMENT

The Brer Rabbit nymph was originally designed to catch trout from waters where the fish could be seen, stalked, and then cast to with a fast-sinking nymph. It also works well early in the season, when it can be trundled along hard on the bottom to imitate a range of creatures, including the caddis larva and alder fly larva.

DRESSING

Hook: Size 8 or 10 long-shank.
Tying silk: Brown.
Lead underbody: Five or six strips of lead-foil bound lengthways along the hook-shank.
Tail: Two goose biot fibres dyed brown.
Body: Brown angora wool.
Rib: Round gold tinsel or wire.
Thorax: Dubbed rabbit fur.
Wing-cases: Hen-pheasant centre-tail.
Hackle: Brown partridge.
Head: Clear varnish.

Brian Gent

Brian, from London, could be described as the 'crafty Cockney'. I meet him regularly at Grafham and Rutland. He is one of the few men to land a double-figure rainbow from a reservoir, and he did it with a 10½lb fish from the Queen Mother Reservoir. He is also one of the neatest fly-tyers I know.

1 Green Muddler Doll

COMMENT

This pattern is my most successful big-fish lure, having accounted for reservoir rainbows of 12lb 2oz and 10lb 1oz, as well as many trout in the 4–5lb bracket. It is at its best in deep water, especially at places such as Datchet and Farmoor II. I normally fish it from an anchored boat on a Hi-Speed Hi-D line and a 22ft leader, inching it along the bottom in depths of 30ft. The white deerhair head keeps it clear of bottom debris.

DRESSING

Hook: Size 6 long-shank.
Tying silk: White.
Body: Fluorescent phosphor-yellow wool.
Head: White deerhair, clipped but left large.

2 Parmachene Belle

COMMENT

This American pattern appeared in my fly-box as a result of experiments with married wings. There it stayed until one late April day at Grafham when I drifted over a shoal of willing stockies. I tied one on and quickly had to leave the shoal for fear of catching a limit too soon. It is now a regular killer when used loch-style on most Midlands reservoirs. Its greatest day was at the last International held at Draycote, when it was the most successful pattern, fished either as a point-fly or on the middle dropper.

DRESSING

Hook: Size 10 to 14 Captain Hamilton medium-weight.
Tying silk: Black.
Tail: Married goose cossette; white, red, white.
Butt: Peacock herl.
Body: Primrose floss.
Rib: Flat gold tinsel.
Wing: Married goose cossette, as tail.
Hackle: Beard hackle of mixed red and white cock.
Head: Black varnish.

1 Green Muddler Doll   **2** Parmachene Belle   **3** Weeney Macsweeney   **4** Gosling
5 All-rounder   **6** Harry Tom   **7** Red Tag Wingless Wickham's   **8** Chief Needabeh

3 Weeney Macsweeney

COMMENT

From the middle of May, most of my fishing is restricted to loch-style from a drifting boat and the remainder of my patterns are geared to this style. The first of them is the Weeney, introduced to me by regular England International, Brian Thomas. It is a terrific early-season fly when fished on the point of a team of three. Fished on a floating line over shallows from the middle of April until the water warms sufficiently for trout to begin surface-feeding in earnest, it is far superior to the original Sweeney Todd and is a first-class fish-taker.

DRESSING

Hook: Size 10 Partridge International extra-heavyweight.
Tying silk: Black.
Tag: Silver wire.
Body: Rear two-thirds, black floss, ribbed silver wire. Front third, fluorescent magenta floss.
Wing: Black squirrel-tail, tied sparse.
Hackle: Scarlet cock (rather long in the fibre) tied as a full collar hackle in front of the wing.
Head: Black varnish.

4 Gosling

COMMENT

I have modified this popular Irish Mayfly pattern to suit the reservoirs I fish, where the lack of natural mayfly hatches in no way diminishes its killing potential. It was introduced to me when my regular boat partner, Mickey Miller, asked me to tie some for an International on Lough Conn. An article in *Trout and Salmon* not only gave me the correct tying, but also mentioned the author's success with the pattern at Grafham. I now use it regularly as a bob-fly during the warmer months, when it is a superb alternative to the ever-popular Soldier Palmer.

DRESSING

Hook: Size 10 and 12.
Tying silk: Brown.
Tail: Four or five strands of bronze mallard.
Body: Yellow seal's fur.
Rib: Oval gold tinsel.
Hackles: Orange cock with a grey mallard hackle in front.
Head: Clear varnish.

5 All-rounder

COMMENT

John Ketley's aptly-named invention has caught fish for me on numerous occasions from early April to late October, but, surprisingly, it never seems to work throughout the day. The style of tying would seem to indicate that the All-rounder should be fished in the bob position, but I have had most success with it fished on the middle dropper, especially when teamed with a bushy Soldier Palmer on the top dropper. Dibbling the Soldier Palmer seems to attract the trout's attention. Then they see the All-rounder and take it, often hooking themselves.

DRESSING

Hook: Size 10 to 14.
Tying silk: Brown.
Body: Brown tying silk.
Body Hackle: Natural red cock, palmered from head to tail.
Rib: Flat gold tinsel.
Wing: Teal flank, rolled.
Hackle: Natural red cock wound as full collar hackle in front of the wing.
Head: Clear varnish.

6 Harry Tom

COMMENT

I came across this Welsh sea-trout pattern at Grafham when Tom Ivens won an England eliminator with 12 trout, most of them taken on the Harry Tom. I begged a couple of flies and noticed that one had a wing of bronze mallard while the other sported a hen-pheasant wing quill as its wing. I tied both versions and since then both have caught consistently on all the reservoirs I fish. They are most successful when fished on the point, but smaller sizes do well on the middle dropper in calm conditions.

DRESSING

Hook: Size 10 to 16 Captain Hamilton medium-weight.
Tying silk: Brown.
Tail: Honey cock hackles.
Body: Blue rabbit fur with a fair number of guard hairs mixed.
Rib: Oval gold.
Hackle: Honey cock.
Wing: Bronze mallard (the original winging material). Hen-pheasant tail or hen-pheasant wing quill is equally effective.
Head: Clear varnish.

7 Red Tag Wingless Wickham's

COMMENT

The Wickham's Fancy often proves more successful without the wings, and this pattern is simply my own variation of the Wingless Wickham's. The addition of a fluorescent red tag undoubtedly enhances its killing prowess, especially in the warmer months. It can work anywhere on the cast, although I favour it as a bob-fly on bright, windy days, while Bob Church swears by it as a point-fly. Indeed, it was his best fish-taking pattern at Rutland in 1984 when fished in this position.

DRESSING

Hook: Size 10 to 16 Captain Hamilton medium-weight.
Tying silk: Brown.
Tag: Seven or eight strands of fluorescent red floss teased out with a needle.
Body: Flat gold tinsel.
Body hackle: Natural red cock palmered from head to tail.
Rib: Oval gold tinsel.
Hackle: Natural red cock.
Head: Clear varnish.

8 Chief Needabeh

COMMENT

This versatile lure has been around for many years, but is rarely seen in the fly-fisher's box. It works throughout the season both fished slowly on a sinking line early on, and on a floater or slow-sink in high summer when, fished just sub-surface, it has accounted for many daphina-feeding rainbows. The fact that hardly anyone carries this pattern, may well be the reason it has proved so successful for me. Even rainbows must get fed-up with Black Lures, Whisky Flies and Muddlers, and so they go for something different when it's put before them.

DRESSING

Hook: Size 6 to 8 long-shank.
Tying silk: Black.
Tag: Flat silver tinsel.
Body: Scarlet floss.
Rib: Oval silver tinsel.
Wings: Two yellow cock hackles back-to-back inside. Two orange cock hackles outside.
Hackle: Yellow cock with red cock in front, both wound as collar hackles.
Cheeks: Jungle cock or substitute.
Head: Black varnish.

Sid Knight

Sid is a professional fly-dresser from Bridgnorth in the West Midlands. He spends a lot of time at the scenic Patshull Park fishery. A fine fly-tyer, he has a number of original patterns to his credit. The eight he has chosen here will give good results throughout the season.

1 The Jezabelle

COMMENT

This lure works well throughout the season. I often tie it with a lead underbody, which enables me to fish very deep, ensuring that the fly is close to the bottom throughout the retrieve. It is then that I have the best results. It is a good change lure when trout are feeding on fry.

DRESSING

Hook: Size 10 or 8 long-shank.
Tying Silk: Black.
Body: White chenille.
Rib: Oval silver 14.
Throat hackle: Hot-orange.
Wing: Four white hen hackles tied matuka-style.
Overwing: Bronze mallard.
Head: Black varnish.

2 Fiery Brown

COMMENT

This wet fly is my favourite for sedge time. There are many wet-fly patterns from which to choose, but this one looks the most realistic to my eye, and I believe it fools the trout more readily than some others. On a large reservoir or loch, try it as the centre dropper in a team of three wets. This position is usually the least effective, but not with the Fiery Brown on, when it regularly out-fishes the point- and bob-fly.

DRESSING

Hook: Size 12, 10 or 8.
Tying silk: Black or brown.
Tail: Golden-pheasant tippets.
Rib: Oval gold 14.
Body: Fiery-brown seal's fur with some fluorescent orange seal's fur mixed in and then dubbed on.
Hackle: Natural red/brown or dyed fiery-brown.
Wing: Dark bronze mallard.
Head: Black or clear varnish.

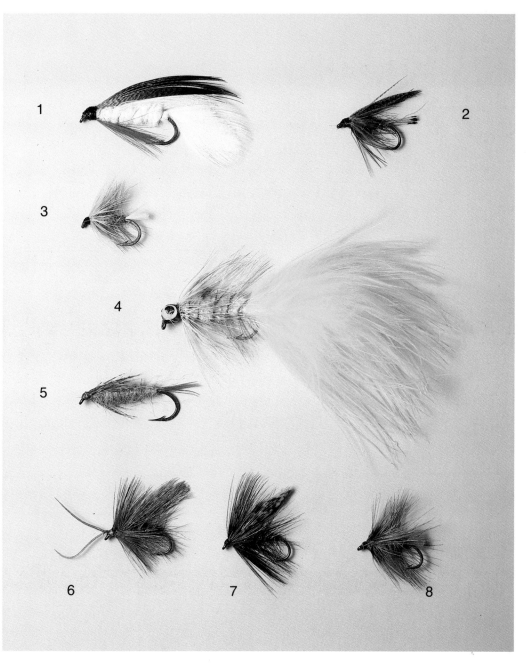

1 The Jezabelle   **2** Fiery Brown   **3** Olive Palmer   **4** Palmered Eyed Dog Nobbler
5 Leaded Damselfly Nymph   **6** Brown Murrough   **7** Black Speckled Sedge
8 Claret Soldier Palmer

3 Olive Palmer

COMMENT

You can begin to use this fly about the third week in May, when a few olives are beginning to hatch. When used in a team of three it is best on the top dropper, where it can be bobbed in the waves. Occasionally I have tried it on the point, then sprayed it with silicone to fish proud on the surface. Coupled with a slow retrieve, it works well when trout are taking adult flies as they float down with the breeze.

DRESSING

Hook: Size 12, 10 or 8 medium-shank.
Tying silk: Black.
Tail: Fluorescent yellow floss.
Body: Dark olive seal's fur ribbed with silver wire.
Body hackle: Palmered light olive cock hackle.
Head hackle: Light olive cock hackle.
Head: Black varnish.

4 Palmered Eyed Dog Nobbler

COMMENT

Although I show a yellow version of Trevor Housby's famous pattern, a complete range can be achieved by changing the colours of the marabou tail and chenille body. The yellow version works particularly well in coloured water, but black is a good early-season pattern. Olive works well when damsel-flies are about, and orange kills when it is hot in mid-summer. White is best when trout are feeding on coarse-fish fry at the back-end.

DRESSING

Hook: Size 8 or mini 8 long-shank.
Tying silk: Black.
Tail: Twice as long as the hook and thick. Any colour (yellow marabou shown).
Rib: Oval silver 14.
Body: Chenille. Any colour.
Palmered hackle: Grizzle.
Head: BB split-shot with painted eyes.

5 Leaded Damselfly Nymph

COMMENT

From late June onwards, this is one of the best imitative patterns I know. I always fish it on the point on a floating line and long leader. It can be fished alone or with other nymph droppers. The naturals swim quite fast on the surface and then crawl up the nearest reed-stem to hatch, so a few non-leaded patterns are advisable for the days when you need to fish the nymphs across the surface.

DRESSING

Hook: Size 12, 10 or 8 long-shank.
Tying silk: Olive.
Underbody: Touching turns of lead wire.
Tail: Cock-pheasant centre-tail fibres.
Rib: Oval gold 14.
Body: Mixed green, olive, orange, yellow and blue seal's fur.
Wing-case: Cock-pheasant centre-tail.
Thorax: As body.
Hackle: Brown partridge.
Head: Clear varnish.

6 Brown Murrough

COMMENT

Although this is a traditional Irish lough pattern imitating some of the larger sedge flies, it has travelled the Irish sea well. Many English reservoir fishers have found it works well as a wake fly on the point or as top dropper. Usually, the bigger the wave, the better this pattern works, for it is highly visible as it skips back through the waves. As well as being a good rainbow-catcher, it will often fool a big brown. Fish it from late June onwards.

DRESSING

Hook: Size 12, 10 or 8.
Tying silk: Black or brown.
Rib: Oval gold 14.
Body: Dark brown seal's fur.
Palmered body hackle: Dark red/brown cock hackle.
Wing: Hen-pheasant centre-tail or any speckled brown feather.
Head hackle: Dark brown cock hackle.
Antennae: Fibres of cock-pheasant centre-tail.

7 Black Speckled Sedge

COMMENT

This may seem a little unusual, but then it's a 'secret weapon'! Bob Church tells me he couldn't go wrong with a size 14 one day on a remote Scottish loch when all else failed. Small dark, almost black, sedges are common on some northern lochs, so if you go to Scotland, make sure you have this pattern in your fly-box. I am told that a size 10 is magic at Grafham and Rutland from July to the season's end.

DRESSING

Hook: 14, 12, 10 or 8.
Tying silk: Black.
Rib: Oval silver 14.
Body: Black seal's fur.
Palmered body hackle: Black cock hackle.
Wing: Speckled-brown hen wing quill.
Head hackle: Black cock hackle.

8 Claret Soldier Palmer

COMMENT

The Soldier Palmer is the most popular top dropper fly, to which, because of its great success, many variations have been introduced. This claret version has been a big success for me and many of my friends, including Bob Church. He tells me it has helped him win a few competitions at Grafham and elsewhere.

DRESSING

Hook: Size 12, 10 or 8.
Tying silk: Black or brown.
Tail: Short, thick fluorescent red floss.
Rib: Oval gold 14.
Body: Blood-red seal's fur, almost light claret.
Palmered body hackle: Natural red/brown cock hackle.
Head hackle: Hen Greenwell.

Raphael Madriago

I met Raphael while I was fishing the rivers Sella and Narcia in northern Spain. Like most of his countrymen, he is a river dry-fly fanatic. However, I am slowly converting him to other tactics when he visits England, and I know he took a sinking line with him on a recent visit to Argentina – and some of my lures. I await his results! Although he now often tries tiny weighted nymphs, Raphael's favourites remain his spider patterns fished on a floating line on or close to the surface.

Although all his flies are tied with sparse, carrot-shaped bodies for the crystal-clear rivers of Spain, they have been found to work well in this country too, especially on the Test and Itchen and on the streams of Yorkshire and Derbyshire. They also do well on our reservoirs, and towards the end of the 1985 season I took two excellent limit-bags on them from Pitsford. My method was to fish them slowly in the surface film in near flat-calm conditions. I was impressed with these early results, especially as the flies are tied so sparsely that it would be easy to disregard them.

1 Red and Black Spider

COMMENT

I have found this pattern as good as any of our English counterparts for early-season buzzer fishing. If you study a close-up colour transparency of an ascending black buzzer nymph, you will clearly see the red-and-black ribbed effect. The artificial, simple as it is, imitates this perfectly. The full, circular hackle also helps to give the impression of the hatching insect, so the fly fishes best on a floating line and lightly greased leader. Retrieve it slowly and evenly with a figure-of-eight action.

DRESSING

Hook: Size 16 or 14.
Tying silk: Black.
Tail: Black hackle whisks.
Body: Half red floss; half black floss.
Hackle: Natural black hen.
Head: Black varnish.

2 Cream Spider

COMMENT

This spider pattern has many imitative uses on stillwaters. It tempted a number of good rainbows during thick caenis hatches at Pitsford during the 1985 summer. A hatch would begin as soon as the water flattened to dead-calm at about mid-evening. I would then remove my three-fly leader, replace it with 3 metres of 3lb breaking-strain nylon straight from the spool, and tie on a Cream Spider. I fished the fly either just sub-surface, where it imitated the nymph, or sprayed and used as a dry fly. The dry-fly version is best fished static.

DRESSING

Hook: Size 16 or 14.
Tying Silk: Primrose.
Tail: Grizzle hackle whisks.
Body: Cream floss ribbed with primrose tying thread.
Hackle: Grizzle hen.
Head: Clear varnish.

1 Red and Black **2** Cream **3** Green **4** Olive
5 Fawn **6** Yellow **7** Orange **8** Grey

7

3 Green Spider

COMMENT

More stillwater trout fisheries seem to be having hatches of olives, which usually begin to appear about the third week in May. Since the olive is a delicate fly, a delicately-tied imitation is needed to deceive the trout, especially if the water is clear. I tried this pattern on both gravel-pit and reservoir fisheries and found takes were confident. It is also effective when those large green buzzers are hatching, which happens at intervals virtually throughout the season – at least, it does on Grafham Water.

DRESSING

Hook: Size 16 or 14.
Tying Silk: Brown.
Tail: Ginger hackle whisks.
Body: Green floss ribbed with brown tying thread.
Hackle: Ginger hen hackle.
Head: Clear varnish.

4 Olive Spider

COMMENT

I used to think there was so much green in nature that any artificial fly or nymph tied in green would blend into the background and be lost from the trout's sight. Now, green, especially olive-green, is one of my favourite colours for wet-fly and nymph patterns. An olive-coloured fly works well when fished so slowly that it is almost static, and if the water is quite clear, so much the better. This Olive Spider has worked well for me at the 'big three': Rutland, Grafham and Pitsford.

DRESSING

Hook: Size 16 or 14.
Tying silk: Olive.
Tail: Olive hen hackle whisks.
Body: Pale olive floss ribbed with olive tying silk.
Hackle: Olive hen.
Head: Clear varnish.

5 Fawn Spider

COMMENT

This fawn-coloured spider looks very much like a mini-mayfly, and although I haven't yet had a chance to try it when the mayfly has been hatching, I bet it would work well. It also bears some similarity to the buff-coloured sedges – the silverhorns, as they are known – and it is during sedge hatches that it is used on the Spanish rivers.

DRESSING

Hook: Size 16 or 14.
Tying silk: Primrose.
Tail: Grizzle hen hackle whisks.
Body: Fawn floss ribbed with primrose tying silk.
Hackle: Grizzle cock.
Head: Clear varnish.

6 Yellow Spider

COMMENT

This is a real all-rounder. You can use it with confidence during a hatch of light olives on a chalk-stream, and you can use it during a sedge hatch on a stillwater. The ascending sedge pupa has quite a lot of yellow in it, and this is particularly noticeable in the 'tangled moment' just before the fly emerges. Fish the Yellow Spider in the surface film from mid-evening onwards from mid-July to September.

DRESSING

Hook: Size 16 or 14.
Tying Silk: Black.
Tail: Blue-dun hackle whisks.
Body: Yellow floss ribbed with black tying silk.
Hackle: Blue-dun hen.
Head: Black varnish.

7 Orange Spider

COMMENT

This pattern is best used in the main summer months, when it catches fish at times of huge daphnia blooms. These blooms occur on many of the rich lowland reservoirs from July through to September, when the daphnia form a major food item for the rainbow trout. The water is then often rusty-orange in colour, and orange fly patterns are deadly. Fish the Orange Spider through the surface film with a fairly fast retrieve

DRESSING

Hook: Size 16 or 14.
Tying silk: Beige.
Tail: Grizzle hen hackle whisks.
Body: Orange floss ribbed with beige tying silk.
Hackle: Grizzle hen.
Head: Clear varnish.

8 Grey Spider

COMMENT

This is a fine imitation of the early-season small, dark buzzer. Try a three-fly cast, all size 14. Put up Grey Spiders on the centre and top droppers, but on the point tie on a Blae and Black to represent the adult hatched fly. Permute the order if takes are slow in coming. For example, try the Blae and Black on the top dropper and grease your leader. If that fails, de-grease your leader with mud, so that the flies fish deeper. Sooner or later, you'll find the correct formula, and good sport should follow.

DRESSING

Hook: Size 16 or 14.
Tying silk: White.
Tail: Grizzle hen hackle whisks.
Body: Grey floss ribbed with white tying silk.
Hackle: Grizzle hen.
Head: Clear varnish.

Bob Morey

When it comes to loch-style fishing, few anglers can touch Bob Morey, from Bedford. He is an absolute master at holding that 'bob-fly' in the waves. He holds the record for the heaviest fish caught in the national Benson and Hedges team event with a brown of 7lb 6oz from Grafham, which was caught on his Peach Doll.

1 Yellow-tailed Wickham's Fancy

COMMENT

This fly is one of the best patterns to use in bright weather and light, gentle breezes. It is always a good fly to have on the cast to start the day. The dressing is for the normal pattern, but the yellow tail does seem to make a difference at times. This fly also works well without the wing when fished dry.

DRESSING

Hook: Size 12 or 10 medium-shank.
Tying silk: Black.
Tail: Yellow duck quill.
Body: Gold tinsel and palmered furnace hackle ribbed with gold.
Wing: Starling.
Head: Black varnish.

2 Fluorescent Green Invicta

COMMENT

A couple of lads I once met had done well on a sedge-pupa type of fly tied with lime-green wool. I tied it as an Invicta, before I'd experimented with the 'yellow-tails'. When Bob Church told me he had once taken all his fish on his Goldie to win a competition, I went home to tie some. However, I used yellow duck quill as the tail and under-wing, and with this fly both Brian Leadbetter and myself got through the eliminators.

DRESSING

Hook: Size 14, 12 or 10 medium-shank.
Tying silk: Black.
Tail: Yellow duck quill.
Body: Fluorescent green floss ribbed with gold wire and palmered with furnace hackle.
Hackle: Blue jay.
Wing: Hen pheasant.
Head: Black varnish.

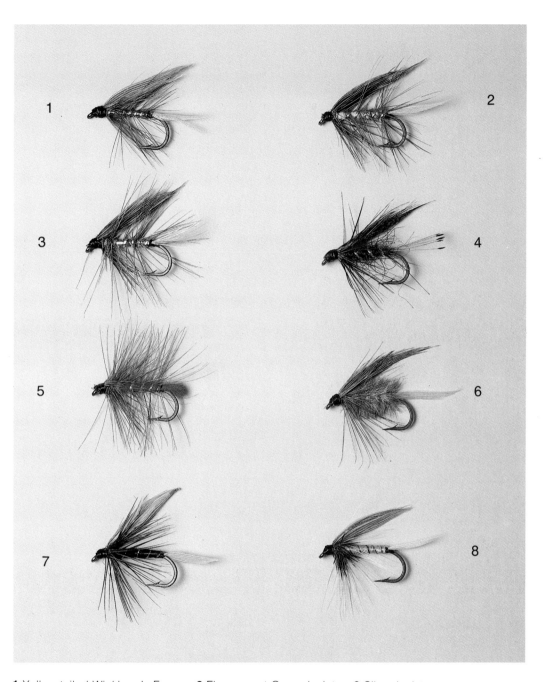

1 Yellow-tailed Wickham's Fancy   2 Fluorescent Green Invicta   3 Silver Invicta
4 Mallard and Claret   5 Fluorescent Soldier Palmer   6 The Green Goddess
7 Winged Black Pennell   8 Yellow-tailed Greenwell's Glory

3 Silver Invicta

COMMENT

The Silver Invicta is one of my favourite point flies, and I feel confident enough to leave it on all day even when the fish are not taking well. Although the fly is worked with yellow golden-pheasant crest, I tried changing to yellow duck and was amazed – I hooked 11 fish in the Midlands final.

DRESSING

Hook: 14, 12 or 10 medium-shank.
Tying silk: Black.
Tail: Yellow golden-pheasant crest or duck.
Body: Silver Lurex ribbed with silver with a furnace palmer hackle to the tail.
Hackle: Blue jay, throat only, tied under the eye.
Wing: Centre hen-pheasant tail.
Head: Black varnish.

4 Mallard and Claret

COMMENT

The Mallard and Claret is another favourite of mine. I have never tried to alter it, and I have taken fish on it when sedges, buzzers or any of the darker-coloured flies have been hatching. I like to use it as the sun goes down, and the wind abates. Then, oily slicks form, and fish head-and-tail on their edges. Fished on the point, a size 12 Mallard and Claret is a killer.

DRESSING

Hook: Size 14, 12 or 10 medium-shank.
Tying silk: Black.
Tail: Tippets.
Body: Claret to crimson seal's fur ribbed with fine gold wire.
Hackle: Black.
Wing: Bronze mallard.
Head: Black varnish.

5 Fluorescent Soldier Palmer

COMMENT

This is my favourite dropper fly for all occasions. I used to tie the Soldier with a scarlet-coloured wool bought from a department store, but I have found that the fluorescent reds seem to work better on dull overcast days. The Soldier Palmer has been tied in many forms, and one version has fluorescent seal's fur and no tail. On days when the fish seem to swirl at the fly and not take, this pattern may just do the trick.

DRESSING

Hook: 14, 12 or 10 medium-shank.
Tying silk: Black.
Tail: Fluorescent red wool.
Body: Red or scarlet fluorescent wool ribbed with fine gold wire. A red hackle is palmered to the tail with a second hackle tied round the eye to form a full-bodied palmered head.
Head: Black varnish.

6 The Green Goddess

COMMENT

I modified the Green Peter into this pattern that I named the Green Goddess. It has proved really effective not only when the sedges are hatching, but in most conditions. I now try this fly on every outing, and it catches a good number of fish.

DRESSING

Hook: Size 12, or 10 medium-shank.
Tying silk: Black.
Tail: Yellow duck quill.
Body: Olive-green ostrich herl, ribbed with gold.
Wing: Centre hen-pheasant tail.
Hackle: Furnace hackle, throat only.
Head: Black varnish.

7 Winged Black Pennell

COMMENT

I have also tied this fly with the yellow duck and have had a great many fish when I have fished it greased-up in buzzer hatches. I like to have a wing on my Pennell patterns.

DRESSING

Hook: Size 14, 12 or 10 medium-shank.
Tying silk: Black.
Tail: Tippet tail or yellow duck.
Body: Black floss ribbed with silver wire.
Hackle: Black hen.
Wing and throat: Two grey hen hackles.
Head: Black varnish.

8 Yellow-tailed Greenwell's Glory

COMMENT

This fly has done really well for me when fished in a fine ripple and sometimes when greased-up and fished in the surface film. I was introduced to it on Loch Leven on a day when it seemed to have outstanding success, and it is from this pattern that my 'yellow-tails' have evolved.

DRESSING

Hook: Size 12 or 10 medium-shank.
Tying silk: Black.
Tail: Yellow duck quill.
Body: Primrose floss ribbed with fine gold wire.
Wing: Starling.
Hackle: Badger.
Head: Black varnish.

Steve Parton

Steve hails from Nottingham, where he spent many years in management with Raleigh Cycles. In 1985 he left to start his own fishing-tackle business, for which, with his original ideas and experience, prospects are looking good. Steve has been a semi-professional fly-dresser for several years and his big catches of trout from Rutland are well known.

1 Pearl Dazzlelure

COMMENT

In February 1985 Bob Church gave me some of this Bobbydazzlelure woven tubing to try, and I spent the season experimenting with it as a substitute for other materials, particularly white chenille and pearl mylar tubing. I found it gave a significantly different and more subtle effect than either of these, which proved rather important. Pearl Dazzlelure proved just right as a fry-imitation body material for days of sunshine and a little ripple. Just wind it on tight and soak it with clear varnish, for a body that is just the right colour and as hard as nails.

DRESSING

Hook: Tadpole Sparton nickel size 6 or 8 long-shank. BB shot jig 4x Mustad 79580 long-shank.
Tying silk: Black.
Tail: White fluorescent marabou with a few strands of Lureflash in the centre.
Rib: Medium silver oval.
Body: Tie in Dazzlelure at head and wind it to bend and back again, taking care to pull it tight. Rib, tie off and don't forget to varnish solidly.
Head: Clear varnish.

2 Sparton Sedge Pupa

COMMENT

I believe trout pay scant regard to the sedge pupa, with but one exception – and this represents it. The pupae start coming in to the bank where they hatch by crawling up weed-stems from the second week in June on the Midlands reservoirs, perhaps a fortnight earlier in Devon and Cornwall. The artificial is best fished as a point-fly and hand-twist retrieved upwind. It is more effective if you begin the retrieve as soon as the flies land, so that the artificial is kept high in the water. Its usefulness is finished by the end of June.

DRESSING

Hook: Partridge L2A 2½× long-shank nymph size 14 or 16.
Tying silk: Black.
Abdomen: Bright Naples yellow swan or goose herl. Black marabou back stripe.
Abdominal rib: Naples yellow Gudebrod fine rod-whipping nylon.
Thorax: Chestnut seal's fur and sepia mink.
Stub wings: Cinnamon duck.
Hackle: One turn of short brown partridge.
Head: Black varnish.

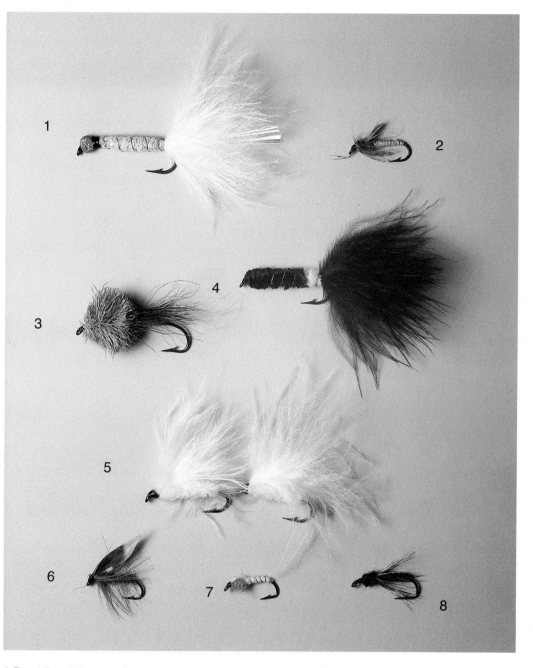

1 Pearl Dazzlelure   **2** Sparton Sedge Pupa   **3** Acme Thunderer   **4** Greenbutting Tadpole
5 White Christmas Tree   **6** Sienna Sedge   **7** Buff Buzzer   **8** Black Emerger

3   Acme Thunderer

COMMENT

This fly is the brainchild of the Dickinson brothers and the late Dave Greaves. Specifically designed for surface-feeding fish on those quiet, drizzly, grey midsummer days we seem to have so often, when the fish are concentrating on Daphnia at the surface, the Acme offers an exciting way of taking trout. It has to be fished greased-up solidly so that it can be bounced over the surface with a dropper 18 inches in front causing it to dip in and then to pop back out, making an enormous disturbance. Fish it to risers and pull it as fast as possible.

DRESSING

Hook: 4× long-shank size 4 or 6.
Tying silk: Black.
Body: Wide copper Lurex.
Rib: Copper wire.
Wing: Grey squirrel.
Head: A large bullet shape trimmed from spun deerhair, preferably red deer.

4   Greenbutting Tadpoles (and Marabou-tailed Crappie Jigs)

COMMENT

Terry Griffiths introduced the leaded Tadpole from which I took the basic colours. I have had success on unlikely days by adding a few strands of pearl Lureflash or Flashabou to the tails. I applied the same process to the Panfish and Crappie Jigs brought from the USA. I made them longer, shortened the tails, reduced the head shot to a BB, and dressed them up in the same way as the Tadpoles. Use the Tadpole exclusively off the bank and for evening and top-water situations from the boat. If you can't see fish rising, use the Leadheads.

DRESSING

Hook: Tadpoles – size 6 or 8 Mustad 3× long-shank or Sparton long-shank. Leadheads – Mustad 4× long-shank, the last ⅛-inch cranked with BB shot Superglued into place.
Tying silk: Black.
Tail: Marabou.
Rib: Fine silver oval.
Butt: Two turns of fluorescent green chenille.
Body: Medium chenille. For the Tadpole bulk up front, wrap extra turns at the eye.
Head: Black varnish.

5   White Christmas Tree

COMMENT

This fly was evolved after Ron Burgin and I had been singing *I'm dreaming of a white Christmas* on the way home from Rutland. I tied a fly using the basic fluorescent additions that were a major part of the attractiveness of the original Christmas Tree in black. I didn't fish with it until the following season when, on a very hot day, Jim Clements put one on and promptly started catching large browns in the middle of Rutland's North Arm. It is still my principal weapon for fishing deep with a white lure, and it has caught more than 1,000 Rutland trout.

DRESSING

Hook: Mustad 3× long-shank size 8 or Sparton Nickel long-shank size 8 in tandem on 25lb Tynex or American Mason nylon.
Tying silk: Black.
Tail: Eight strands of arc-chrome fluorescent orange floss.
Body: White fluorescent medium chenille.
Rib: Medium oval tinsel.
Wings: White fluorescent marabou.
Cheeks: One thickness of Sparton Target Green wool.
Head: Black varnish.

6 Sienna Sedge

COMMENT

This is a generally effective fly. It was inspired by Tony Knight's Tobacco Sedge, popularised by Bob Carnill as the Shredge. I turned the basic idea into a traditional palmer which would represent the hatching ginger buzzers so common on English reservoirs in summer. With a sienna seal's fur body as the basis, the rest was easy. There aren't many small-fly days from June to late September when I don't have one on my cast. This fly is almost an English version of the classic Irish fly, the Fiery Brown.

DRESSING

Hook: Any wet-fly size 10, 12 or 14.
Tying silk: Black.
Body: Sienna seal's fur.
Rib: Fine gold oval.
Throat and body hackle: Red game-cock, palmered.
Wing: Hen-pheasant secondary, oak turkey or grouse. I carry all three variations to cope with fractional differences in hatches.
Head: Black varnish.

7 Buff Buzzer

COMMENT

I tied this fly for no good reason other than to use up some condor I had been given 15 years before. It has proved itself as a general nymph/pupa pattern for high-summer evenings time and time again. I have no idea what trout mistake it for – perhaps a smallish sedge pupa, perhaps a Caenis nymph. It is best fished on the middle dropper of a long nymphing leader, Cove-style, and hand-twisted for the retrieve. It occasionally works in late evening when thrown at a riser and twitched off its nose.

DRESSING

Hook: Sproat bend size 10, 12, 14 or 16.
Tying silk: Black.
Body: Swan or goose dyed palest beige. Dye it yourself and aim for an off-white shade.
Rib: Fine gold wire.
Thorax: Seal's fur dyed beige (a gingery-pink) and dubbed into a ball with the butts of the body pulled over as a wing-case and trimmed off short after whip-finishing.
Head: Black varnish.

8 Black Emerger

COMMENT

This fly came about specifically as a result of my reading Swisher and Richards' classic work, *Selective Trout*. The book points out that trout can be preoccupied with a specific stage of a particular insect, so I set out to see if the theory held good with buzzers. After a season or so I concluded that it probably did, but even if it didn't, at least I had found one pattern that actually worked on the middle dropper – above the pupa and below the quill. I would extend the range significantly to cope with later hatches if I did more bank fishing.

DRESSING

Hook: Sproat bend size 10 or 12.
Tying silk: Black.
Body: Black mole dubbed tight.
Rib: Stripped black peacock quill or polythene strip, which is just as good.
Mid-hackle: Two turns of badger cock raked back almost flat.
Thorax: A pronounced dubbed ball of black mole.

45

Alan Pearson

Everyone knows Alan, who comes from a tiny Buckinghamshire village called Lillingstone Lovell. He is the current British title-holder for the heaviest rainbow at 19lb 8oz and the heaviest brook trout at 5lb 13½oz. Both fish came from the famous Avington fishery in Hampshire.

1 Twitchett Nymph

COMMENT

This is a remarkable trout killer, particularly when plenty of feeding fish may be seen, but seem 'picky' about taking any artificial flies. It is often effective as point-fly to a team of buzzers, and it works well in the same position fished loch-style from a drifting boat. It is possibly most effective when slightly weighted and fished alone on a long, fine leader, when it should be retrieved in a series of short twitches. It is named after a lady friend of my youth, Miss Twitchett.

DRESSING

Hook: Size 10, 12 or 14 long-shank.
Tying silk: Brown.
Underbody: Fine copper wire or lead wire if required.
Body: Pheasant-tail fibres tied slim and ending roughly opposite hook-point.
Thorax: Natural rabbit fur tied slim.
Hackle: Ginger hen.
Tail: Slim bunch of signal-green DF floss extending just beyond bend and cut square.
Head: Clear varnish.

2 White Capper

COMMENT

Streamer lures have wings tied in over the back; Nobbler-type lures have the wings transferred to the tail. The Capper has wings tied in at the sides to add width and enhance visual appeal. Colours can be varied to include black, orange, yellow, pink and a variety of two-colour combinations. The pattern can be fished leaded on a floating line or unleaded on a sinking line, with a slow, steady retrieve. The first season it was used it accounted for more than 300 trout by the end of April. Because of its high visibility, it catches a great many trout.

DRESSING

Hook: Size 6, 8 or 10 Draper nymph hook.
Tying silk: Black.
Underbody: Tying silk. Lead wire may be added if required.
Body: Flat silver tinsel.
Wings: White marabou plume tied in as three pairs on opposing sides of the body.
Tail: White marabou plume.
Head: Black varnish.

1 Twitchett Nymph   **2** White Capper   **3** Damselfly Nymph   **4** Grizzly Beetle
5 Green Beast   **6** Black Wonderbug   **7** Mayfly Nymph   **8** Shrimp

3 Damselfly Nymph

COMMENT

This version of the Damselfly Nymph is particularly suited to the Avington style of nymphing to observed trout, especially when the maximum number of lead strips are tied into the underbody. Reducing the amount of lead permits it to be fished in any water where the natural exists in quantity and one is fishing at random. Floating-line techniques are preferred, and a reduction in weight will allow the use of longer leaders, perhaps up to five yards. The retrieve should be in short, jerky pulls, causing the nymph to adopt a darting action.

DRESSING

Hook: Size 8 long-shank.
Tying silk: Light brown or olive.
Underbody: Up to seven strips of lead-foil.
Body: Mixture of green, yellow and brown wool or seal's fur.
Tail and wing-cases: Pheasant-tail fibres.
Hackle: Pale speckled partridge.
Ribbing: Tying silk.
Head: Clear varnish.

4 Grizzly Beetle

COMMENT

This is a general-purpose pattern which can be used to simulate a great many insects on which trout feed. An unweighted version may be greased-up and fished as a dry fly, in which case it can be effective when the smaller sedges are up. Allowed to sink into or just beneath the surface film, it is often effective when chironomids are hatching. Fished deeper, it can represent water-beetles, shrimps and perhaps the hoglouse. It comes into its own when no consistent feeding pattern is apparent and trout are taking all manner of food.

DRESSING

Hook: Size 8 or 10 standard-shank.
Tying silk: Black.
Underbody: May be weighted with fine lead or copper wire.
Body: Black ostrich herl wound fairly fat.
Hackle: Grizzle cock hackle wound palmer style.
Back: Pheasant-tail fibres tied to splay out the palmered hackle, leaving some hackle-fibres pointing back to form tail.
Head: Black varnish.

5 Green Beast

COMMENT

This is the original and most effective Green Beast tying. Initially intended to represent the larval form of a large water-beetle, it also serves as a general-purpose pattern to imitate other creatures. It is a good pattern for offering to observed feeding trout in clear-water fisheries, and has accounted for a good many 'doubles'. It is best fished on a floating or intermediate line, and the most successful retrieve style seems to be a slow, steady figure-of-eight. It catches trout most consistently from June onwards.

DRESSING

Hook: Size 8 long-shank.
Tying silk: Green.
Underbody: Lead wire or foil.
Body: Grass-green floss.
Tail: Cock hackle-fibres matching body colour.
Rib: Fine silver wire.
Hackle: Long-fibred dark speckled partridge tied sparsely.
Head: Clear varnish.

6 Black Wonderbug

COMMENT

The Wonderbug was an attempt to create a standardised nymph-tying which accentuated all the important recognition factors, and with which any nymph could be simulated merely by changing hook-size and colour. The thorax has been enlarged and the hackle is tied in at the junction of thorax and abdomen, slanting steeply back over the abdomen. Cock hackle tends to trap air-bubbles between itself and the body dubbing, which lends translucency. Fish it according to the nymph being imitated.

DRESSING

Hook: Size 8 long-shank.
Tying silk: Black.
Underbody: Fine lead wire under thorax.
Body: Black seal's fur or substitute mixed with small pinch of scarlet.
Wing-cases, hackle and tail: Black cock hackle-fibres.
Head: Black varnish.

7 Mayfly Nymph

COMMENT

This is possibly the greatest killer of large trout ever devised. The brainchild of Richard Walker, it came into prominence at Avington and other small clear-water fisheries where large trout could be located visually at great depths and where it was essential to attain the required depth as quickly as possible while offering a realistic imitation of a natural food. Trout of all sizes and species accept it readily even where the natural does not exist. It is best fished on a floating line with a leader of up to four yards.

DRESSING

Hook: Size 8 long-shank.
Tying silk: Brown.
Underbody: Up to seven strips of foil.
Body: Pale buff wool.
Tail, wing-cases and legs: Pheasant-tail fibres.
Ribbing: Brown silk.
Cilia: Body material picked out along sides.
Head: Clear varnish.

8 Shrimp

COMMENT

A great many different shrimp tyings exist, but this version is an extremely consistent catcher of rainbow and brown trout in large or small lakes, rivers or streams. The lead strip being secured to the back of the shank means that the fly fishes upside down – essential when prospecting around weedbeds. Colour mixes of dark brown and black are useful, especially in coloured water. The colour mix given is most effective in summer and autumn. Allow the nymph to sink to the required depth in stillwater and then retrieve it in short pulls.

DRESSING

Hook: Size 8 or 10 standard-shank.
Tying silk: Green.
Underbody: Lead strip secured to back of hook-shank.
Body: Mixture of green, yellow and brown wool or seal's fur.
Hackle: Long-fibred clear gingery cock hackle wound palmer fashion.
Back: Tie in a narrow strip of clear polythene or clip the hackle close over the back and varnish.
Head: Black varnish.

Irish Flies

What a great collection this is – absolute 'musts' if you go to Ireland to fish the famous limestone loughs. The Murrough, in its colours of claret, brown and grey, and the Green Peter are probably Ireland's most prolific trout-catchers. Why Ireland's sedges are so much larger than those in Britain I am not sure, but I do know that these two patterns imitate them very well. Then there is the Golden Olive, a fly I would normally favour in its small sizes. However, big Tom O'Reilly, from Belfast, won the World Wet-fly Championship a few years ago using a long-shank size 8. This was on Lough Mask, but he found the large pattern also killed on Lough Carra. The important thing about all these flies is they have travelled well and are now great favourites on this side of the Irish Sea, too.

1 Green Wet Mayfly

COMMENT

This pattern imitates the Mayfly nymph as it is about to emerge. The natural nymph swims quite quickly to the surface when it is about to hatch, so this artificial often produces good results when fished fairly fast. However, it is always a good idea to allow the fly to hang static for a second or two before lifting off to re-cast.

DRESSING

Hook: Size 10 or 8 medium-shank.
Tying silk: Black.
Tail: Pheasant-tail feather-fibres.
Body: Yellowy-green floss, wool or seal's fur ribbed with gold wire.
Hackle: Speckled grey mallard dyed green.
Head: Black varnish.

2 Connemara Black

COMMENT

This basically black fly has flashes of bright colour blended into its dressing. It originates from that most beautiful part of Ireland where the large limestone loughs give such good sport with brown trout. I have found it a good general all-season pattern. It can fool fish which are on the black chironomid or taking dark sedges, and it is as popular on this side of the Irish Sea as it is in the west of Ireland. It is a good point-fly and a good centre dropper, and reservoir rainbows and Scottish loch wild browns go for it as well. It must be in your box.

DRESSING

Hook: Size 14, 12 or 10.
Tying silk: Black.
Tail: Golden-pheasant crest.
Body: Black seal's fur or wool ribbed with fine oval silver tinsel.
Hackle: Black cock and blue jay mixed.
Wing: Bronze mallard.
Head: Black varnish.

1 Green Wet Mayfly   **2** Connemara Black   **3** Bibio   **4** Cock Robin
5 Sooty Olive   **6** Green Peter   **7** Claret Murrough   **8** Golden Olive

3 Bibio

COMMENT

In April and early May many small black chironomids appear on the Irish loughs. They are locally nicknamed 'Duckfly'. A size 14 or 12 Bibio is a good pattern to have on your cast during this period. The larger sizes, 10 or 8, are best tried as top droppers during a big wave when boat-fishing in traditional style.

DRESSING

Hook: Size 14, 12, 10 or 8.
Tying silk: Black.
Body: Black seal's fur or wool with a bright red central blob and ribbed with silver oval thread.
Body hackle: Palmered black cock.
Head: Black varnish.

4 Cock Robin

COMMENT

This is one of the lesser-known Irish patterns which must be termed a fancy fly. Robert McHaffie introduced me to it at the Game Fair some six years ago, telling me to try it on the western loughs. I have caught few trout on it, but friends have done better. My best results with it were in fact at Grafham – at sedge time believe it or not.

DRESSING

Hook: Size 14, 12 or 10.
Tying silk: Black.
Tail: Golden-pheasant tippet dyed red.
Body: Rear half, red seal's fur; front half, light brown seal's fur ribbed with gold wire.
Hackle: Honey cock.
Wing: Bronze mallard.
Head: Black varnish.

5 Sooty Olive

COMMENT

Among the most common small flies to hatch on the Irish loughs are the olives. These delicate upwinged flies vary from light to dark, but it is this dark artificial which Irish fly-fishers favour most. I often use it as my centre dropper, and on the right day it works well. One early August day I did extremely well with it on Lough Carra and finished up with three Sooty Olives on my cast. The Sooty works well on English reservoirs, especially when fished lough-style.

DRESSING

Hook: Size 14, 12 or 10.
Tying silk: Black.
Tail: Golden-pheasant tippets.
Body: Dark olive seal's fur or substitute ribbed with gold wire.
Hackle: Black cock.
Wing: Bronze mallard.
Head: Black varnish.

6 Green Peter

COMMENT

I rate this fly highly and have had good results with it on Loughs Mask, Conn and Carra. It makes a good centre dropper. This position usually attracts fewest fish, but not so with the Green Peter. If trout are really going for it, I fish a size 12 on the point, a size 10 in the centre, and a Murrough or Mayfly on the top dropper. Green-coloured sedges are common on all the great limestone loughs in mid- to late summer. The Green Peter works well at sedge time on English and Welsh reservoirs, and on the Scottish lochs.

DRESSING

Hook: Size 12, 10 or 8 medium-shank.
Tying silk: Black.
Body: Varying shades of green seal's fur, ribbed with fine gold oval tinsel.
Wing: Speckled pheasant feather or substitute. The Irish use a prominent rolled wing.
Hackle: Prominent and fully circular ginger or medium-brown hen tied in after the wing.
Head: Black varnish.

7 Claret Murrough

COMMENT

This claret version of the Murrough has been my most successful fly on recent mid-summer trips to Ireland. I usually fish it as my top dropper, but in a big wave I use it on the point as well. I cast further than is traditional for the Irish loughs, but I do get a lot of takes on the retrieve just as happens with Muddlers fished for English reservoir rainbows. This is a good reservoir fly at sedge time.

DRESSING

Hook: Size 10 or 8.
Tying silk: Black.
Body: Claret seal's fur dubbed generously and ribbed with gold oval tinsel.
Wing: Prominent rolled wing of brown turkey or substitute.
Hackle: Medium-brown cock wound generously and tied in after wing.
Head: Black varnish.

8 Golden Olive

COMMENT

This is a first-class all-round wet-fly pattern. As well as imitating the various olives that begin to hatch in mid-May, it also does well on the days when olive chironomids are hatching. In its larger sizes it can also represent the olive/yellow coloration of a Mayfly. It is a good change-fly at times when a Greenwell's or an Olive Quill is being used. Certainly our larger reservoir trout are regularly deceived by this pattern.

DRESSING

Hook: Size 14, 12, 10 or 8.
Tying silk: Black.
Tag (optional): Orange floss.
Tail: Golden-pheasant crest or olive hackle-fibres.
Body: Olive seal's fur ribbed with fine gold oval tinsel.
Hackle: Golden-olive cock.
Wing: Brown mallard shoulder.
Head: Black varnish.

Sea Trout Favourites

This is a selection for both loch and river, and some are good brown trout patterns as well. My favourites for night-fishing on the rivers are the Squirrel and Silver, Stoat's Tail and Watson's Fancy. The Kingfisher Butcher is a good point-fly for the lochs, with Silver Doctor, Heckham Peckham, Black and Orange and Peter Ross being good all-rounders. It's difficult to imagine anything more exciting than wading a river in the dark, casting away for perhaps an hour, and then having the inevitable powerhouse take. If your doctor has warned you not to get too excited, you'd better not go after sea trout at night. They are terrific!

1 Silver Doctor

COMMENT

An excellent sea trout fly, this slimmed-down version has scored well on the Welsh rivers. It seems to work best on a sinking line at night, and has been the downfall of known big fish resting in deep pools at times of low water.

DRESSING

Hook: Size 12, 10 or 8.
Tying silk: Black.
Tail: Golden-pheasant tippet.
Body: Silver tinsel ribbed with silver wire.
Hackle: Kingfisher-blue cock.
Wing: Grey feather-fibre.
Head: Black varnish.

2 Kingfisher Butcher

COMMENT

This is a great trout fly when fished on the point of a team of wets. I use it in sizes 14 and 12 in a light breeze, but in a higher wave a size 10 is better. I feel confident fishing it for rainbows or browns in reservoirs or Scottish lochs, and I am told that it is an excellent sea trout fly and has the reputation of tempting the larger fish at night.

DRESSING

Hook: Size 14, 12, 10 or 8.
Tying silk: Black.
Tail: Kingfisher-blue hackle-fibres.
Body: Gold tinsel ribbed with gold wire.
Hackle: Hot-orange.
Wing: Blue-black mallard.
Head: Black varnish.

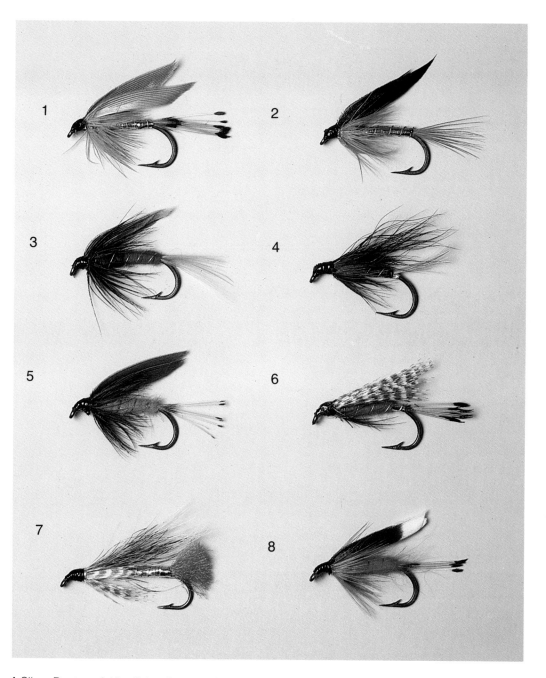

1 Silver Doctor **2** Kingfisher Butcher **3** Watson's Fancy **4** Stoat's Tail
5 Black and Orange **6** Peter Ross **7** Squirrel and Silver **8** Heckham Peckham

3 Watson's Fancy

COMMENT

This fancy fly, invented by Donald Watson of Inverness, was originally intended for catching brown trout, and in this respect it has long proved its worth on all the major Scottish lochs. It has also been favoured south of the Border, and many well-known reservoir men often have a Watson's on their cast. It is also one of the best sea trout flies I know, catching lots of fish in Ireland while being fished from a drifting boat on those Co. Galway loughs.

DRESSING

Hook: Size 12, 10 or 8.
Tying silk: Black.
Tail: Golden-pheasant crest.
Body: Rear half, red; front half, black. Use floss wool or seal's fur ribbed with fine silver oval tinsel.
Hackle: Black cock.
Wing: Crow wing.
Eyes (optional): Jungle cock if you have it, or jungle cock substitute.
Head: Black varnish.

4 Stoat's Tail

COMMENT

If you are fishing for sea trout with the Stoat's Tail and a salmon is about, it will take this fly in preference to any other – at least, that has been my experience while fishing shallow, clear rivers. It is an excellent fly for sea trout in that hour as dusk approaches, when many anglers like to rest a pool. In fact, it has great all-round appeal and seems to work well on all game-rivers. Yes, it is a good trout fly as well!

DRESSING

Hook: Size 12, 10 or 8.
Tying silk: Black.
Tail: Golden-pheasant crest.
Tag: Silver wire.
Body: Black floss ribbed with silver wire.
Hackle: Black cock.
Wing: Black stoat's-tail hair or squirrel as a substitute.
Head: Black varnish.

5 Black and Orange

COMMENT

This fly seems to work best in its larger sizes. It has been responsible for the downfall of many big fish on the rivers of North Wales, and it fishes well on a sunk line when takes come at the tail of a pool.

DRESSING

Hook: Size 10 or 8.
Tying silk: Black.
Tail: Golden-pheasant tippet.
Body: Orange seal's fur or substitute ribbed with copper wire.
Hackle: Black hen.
Wing: Bronze mallard.
Head: Black varnish.

6 Peter Ross

COMMENT

This famous fly has never done much for me, and is the one in which I have least confidence. On occasions when rainbows have been on and easy to catch, I have joked with my fishing companion, saying, 'I know how to stop this. I'll put on a Peter Ross!' Sure enough, the fishing has ground to a halt! Having said that, I have to admit that I have caught a few decent sea trout on the pattern while river fishing. And on Lough Innagh in the west of Ireland, four of us drift-fishing with size 12 flies caught a good bag of fish of which most were taken on the Peter Ross.

DRESSING

Hook: Size 14, 12, 10 or 8.
Tying silk: Black.
Tail: Golden-pheasant tippet.
Body: Tail half, silver tinsel; front half, bright red seal's fur. Both ribbed with silver oval tinsel.
Hackle: Black cock.
Wing: Teal.
Head: Black varnish.

7 Squirrel and Silver

COMMENT

This pattern was first shown to me by John McLellan at Eyebrook and Pitsford in 1963. It was a good lure for both rainbow and brown trout on these waters. Bank tactics were to cast a long line (silk in those days), allow the lure to sink well down, and to make a steady retrieve. Later, it was found that the Squirrel and Silver worked well on other reservoirs, including Grafham and Rutland, where specialised sinking-line boat tactics were developed. It was in the early 1970s that I found this lure was a deadly sea trout pattern.

DRESSING

Hook: Size 12, 10, 8 or 6.
Tying silk: Black.
Tail: Red wool or hackle-fibres.
Body: Silver tinsel.
Hackle: Silver mallard fibres.
Wing: Natural squirrel-tail.
Head: Black varnish.

8 Heckham Peckham

COMMENT

William Murdoch, of Aberdeen, devised this now well-known fly, which he first used for catching sea trout on the Scottish east-coast rivers. It is now a proven sea trout favourite throughout these islands, and not a bad trout fly. To be certain of a perfect pair of wings, make sure you cut your feather-fibre from corresponding quills of the white-tipped feather.

DRESSING

Hook: Size 12, 10 or 8.
Tying silk: Black.
Tail: Golden-pheasant tippet.
Body: Red wool or seal's fur ribbed with silver wire.
Hackle: Dark brown hen.
Wing: White-tipped mallard drake.
Head: Black varnish.

Lures

Introduction to Lures

Lures are usually tied on long-shank hooks in sizes 10, 8, 6 and 4. They may be on singles or on two hooks linked as prepared mounts called tandems. Lures have two basic roles: the first is to deceive the trout into taking something that appears to be a natural food; the second is to arouse the trout's aggressive instincts and to provoke it into attacking.

The deceiver type of lure imitates a small coarse-fish fry or a stickleback. Well-known patterns are the Appetiser, Jack Frost, Jersey Herd, Badger Matuka and Missionary; and the new buoyant Ethafoam and pearl lures, with their Flashabou wings, come into this category. Most of the black-based lures can also be classed as deceivers, because when they are fished slow and deep, they are taken for bottom-crawling larvae or leeches. Patterns such as the Ace of Spades, Sweeney Todd, Black Chenille, Christmas Tree and Viva rarely fail when fished on a sinking line.

The attractor patterns are rather more gaudy and flashy. The Whisky Fly, Mickey Finn, Leprechaun, Dunkeld, Orange Muddler and Breathaliser come into this category, as do the new luminous and phosphorescent Flashabou lures, the Frog and Dog Nobblers, the Puppies and Ugly Ducklings. All these patterns are fished fast to excite the aggressive instincts of rainbow trout, which are markedly more noticeable in July, August and early September.

I have included a number of very large lures, which, believe me, are very successful. Some, such as Julian's Rutland Lure, a tube-fly, have been known to catch their creators (in this case Julian Hubbard) more than 400 trout from the Rutland boats in a season, many of them fish of specimen size. Apart from tubes, tandem lures do well when fished on lead-core lines from boats on the large reservoirs. Fred Wagstaffe's giant tandem is probably as large as you would want to go for trout.

Many lures are not difficult to tie. An example is the Orange Chenille (*see* page 89 for dressing), and it's a good one with which to start if you have not tied one before. This is the method. Place a size 6 long-shank hook firmly in the vice, so that the point is masked by the jaws, and thread the black tying silk on to the bobbin-holder. Starting at the eye, trap the tying silk by winding it tightly back on itself and then wind it clockwise along the shank until you reach the hook-bend. If you have done this correctly, you can now release the bobbin-holder, leaving it hanging about three inches below the hook. The weight of the holder ensures that your first simple but most important operation stays secure.

The next job is to tie in the tail of the lure. Take a hackle from your orange cape and tear off a spray of hackle-fibres. Even them up and then tie them directly on top of the hook-shank, using the same clockwise winding action. Having done that, release the bobbin and trim off the surplus material.

You are now ready for the body. Select a 4-inch length of orange chenille and a similar length of gold tinsel. Remove about ¼ inch from the pile of the chenille, leaving the centre core exposed. Tie this in where the tail ends. Now tie in the gold tinsel in the same position, but before doing so, cut the end to a wedge-shaped point. Use about four turns of the tying silk for each operation. Make sure all is secure – and that means using the correct pressure in winding the silk. Pull too hard and the silk will break, and you will have to start again. Cut off the waste chenille and tinsel stubs. Now take the tying silk and bobbin back down close the the eye-end of the hook-shank and again leave the bobbin hanging.

Now wind on the orange chenille, keeping it even and tight. When you reach the tying silk, secure the chenille with four firm turns and cut off the scrap. Leave the bobbin hanging while you go back to the gold tinsel. Wind this anticlockwise in even spirals over the chenille as far as the silk. Tie it in and cut off the scrap.

The next operation is to tie in the throat hackle. Tear off a spray of orange hackle-fibres as you did for the tail, arrange them evenly, and then tie them in beneath the hook-shank. Some vices have a rotating head to make this operation easier, but a little practice will show that such a device is not essential. Cut off the surplus hackle and build up the head section so that it lies evenly to receive the wing.

For the wing, select four even orange cock hackles from your cape and place them together in two pairs so that their shiny sides are facing outwards. Now tie them in so that they are positioned centrally straight along the top of the hook-shank. Keep the wing length such that it finishes at about the same distance as the end of the tail. Cut off the wing waste of the hackle-stalks and form a good-shaped head with the tying silk. Make sure it is not ugly and bulky. A bad head is the most common mistake made by a newcomer to fly-tying. Hold the silk under tension and pull off about twelve inches from the bobbin, taking care that nothing unwinds. Now, instead of a whip finish, tie three simple double half-hitch knots on top of each other. These will hold everything securely. Finally, cut off the waste silk and finish the head by applying a blob of varnish right on the top with the point of your dubbing needle.

Tandem mounts should always be made-up and varnished before a serious tying session. They are fairly easy to assemble, and this is how to set about the job. Select the hooks — usually size 6 long-shank, but you can use size 8 or 4 — and for the connecting link cut off a length of 30lb breaking-strain nylon. Thread one end of the nylon through the eye of a hook and tie a half-hitch knot. Pull this back so that it acts as a stopper at the eye. Cut the nylon level with the hook-bend, and then whip it tightly on to the shank.

Thread the second hook on to the nylon and tie another half-hitch so that it comes to rest about half-way along the shank of the second hook. Whip this tightly on to the shank, double it back on itself, and whip it tightly again, finally trimming off the nylon at the bend of the leading hook. The gap between the hooks should be no more than half an inch. Coat the whole rig generously with clear varnish and allow it to dry. It pays to make up several rigs at one sitting and actually to tie the lures another evening.

Another method, and one which Stuart Billam uses for his Scorpion (see page 18), employs a treble and a single hook. For this, take a piece of 20lb nylon mono-filament, place it along the shank of a treble hook (which has first had the eye closed with a pair of pliers), round the bend and back along the shank on the opposite side. Bind the nylon securely to the shank of the hook with tying silk. Continue past the hook and bind about an inch of the nylon together.

Next, take a single hook and starting ⅛ inch from the eye of the hook wind the tying silk to the bend. Then bind the two thicknesses of nylon along the top of the shank, leaving a protruding tail of about one inch. When you get to within a ¼ inch of the eye of the single, cut off one of the strands of nylon, pass the remaining length of nylon through the eye of the single, back down underneath the hook-shank, and bind it securely. Continue with the nylon past the bend of the single and bind it to the two lengths of nylon. Continue as far as the treble hook. The mount can then be dressed as appropriate.

In days gone by, anglers used to call tandem lures 'Demons', and three-hook lures 'Terrors'. The Americans call lures 'Streamers'. Indeed, this is what I called my first lure creations in the early 1960s. Today, the name lure is readily accepted and most anglers use them at one time or another during a season. When I first wrote of my success with lures at Ravensthorpe in 1964, my Church Fry pattern was looked upon as an invention of the devil. We have come a long way in just two decades.

61

Fish-imitating Lures I

This selection incorporates some of the best fish-imitating lures. Some anglers dedicate themselves to fishing for big trout only, and these are the men who use such lure patterns most of all. Successful lure fishing entails searching the greater depths of our large reservoirs for much of the season. Some anglers say this is boring fishing, but such persistence brings the really heavyweight catches and often the largest specimens. In autumn the larger trout move out of the deeps into the shallower, weedy areas where the new coarse-fish fry congregate. Some of the patterns described here brought good results for me and my friends in the 1970s, and they are still going strong today.

1   White Muddler Minnow

COMMENT

This is a good pattern and one that has caught me some worthwhile rainbows and browns of more than 5lb from Grafham and other large reservoirs. It became my favourite bank lure for when fish were on fry. I clearly remember fishing it off the Plummer car park at Grafham as long ago as 1967. A big brown was crashing into the stickleback shoals. I covered one of his lunging attacks well and he took with confidence. Five minutes later I landed my first 5lb brown trout – a fine fish of 5lb 1oz. It was full of sticklebacks.

DRESSING

Hook: Size 10, 8, 6 or 4 long-shank.
Tying silk: Black.
Tail: White feather-fibre.
Body: Silver tinsel ribbed with silver wire.
Hackle: White cock.
Wing: White feather-fibre, e.g. goose.
Head: White deerhair.
Head finish: Black varnish.

2   Church Fry

COMMENT

I developed this lure at Ravensthorpe during the early 1960s, a time when lures and sinking fly-lines were regarded with suspicion. Good-sized brown trout were feeding on perch fry, and I noticed how they selected one victim and hounded it until it was caught. My idea was to create a rather gaudy version of the perch fry – one that would stand out in a crowd. It worked, and over the years it has proved a good general lure. Richard Walker liked it and named it the Church Fry.

DRESSING

Hook: Size 10, 8 or 6 long-shank bronze.
Tying silk: Black.
Tail: White cock hackle-fibres.
Body: Orange chenille ribbed with gold tinsel.
Hackle: Hot-orange or red cock fibres. Throat only.
Wing: A bunch of natural squirrel-tail hair.
Head: Black varnish.

1 White Muddler Minnow **2** Church Fry **3** Perch Fry **4** Jack Frost Lure
5 Original Baby Doll **6** Muddler Minnow **7** Badger Matuka **8** Missionary

3 Perch Fry

COMMENT

Together with roach, perch are the most common small coarse fish in our large reservoirs. They form an important food-item for both rainbow and brown trout and many patterns have been developed to imitate them. This is one of the older dressings. It may be fished with confidence around shallow weed-beds, boat jetties, valve towers, and other features known to harbour shoals of small perch. Big trout will be close by, and occasionally one will make a mistake.

DRESSING

Hook: Size 12, 8 or 6 long-shank.
Tying silk: Black.
Tail: Golden-pheasant tippet.
Body: Gold tinsel ribbed with gold wire.
Hackle: Bright red. Throat only.
Wing: Four grizzle or cree cock hackles.
Head: Black varnish.

4 Jack Frost Lure

COMMENT

I designed this lure for Grafham in the early 1970s, but it has since proved to work everywhere. Rainbows have a great liking for it, and even the giants of the small fisheries take it when it is fished slowly. Use it on floating, sink-tip or sinking fly-lines.

DRESSING

Hook: Size 10, 8 or 6 long-shank bronze.
Tying silk: White.
Tail: Red wool.
Body: Underbody of white fluorescent wool as in the Baby Doll. Overbody of stretched clear polythene strip.
Wing: Generous spray of white marabou.
Hackle: Two fully-circular turns of scarlet cock; then, close to the eye, three full turns of long-fibred white cock. Tie the hackle in at the roots so that it slopes back.
Head: Clear varnish.

5 Original Baby Doll

COMMENT

One of the best-known patterns of the last twenty years, this was devised by Brian Kench. Trout go absolutely crazy for it at times, but on other occasions they will only follow. If you visit a comparatively newly-stocked water, try this pattern first. Fish it on a sinking or sink-tip fly-line until summer, when a floater is better.

DRESSING

Hook: Size 10, 8 or 6 long-shank.
Tying silk: White or black.
Tail and body: Lay 9 inches of fluorescent white wool along hook-shank as a loop facing eye. Leave a 1-inch single strand and a 1-inch loop projecting at tail. Secure both with silk and take silk down to eye. Loop single strand over back of long loop. Build up a slim body and secure. Pull long loop tight and tie in. Finish head. Cut tail loop to ½ inch and shred.
Head: Clear or black varnish.

6 Muddler Minnow

In early autumn the Muddler Minnow fished on the surface sometimes produces fantastic results with reservoir rainbows. I use a larger head than the original pattern at this time of year, especially if a good wind is blowing. Use a 9 or 10 floating shooting-head to flat nylon backing. Cast as far as you can down-wind. Pause for a second or two, then strip back as fast as you can in long pulls. The popping action of the head hitting the oncoming waves draws fish from deep down and makes for some exciting sport.

Hook: Size 6, 8 or 10 long-shank bronze.
Tying silk: Black.
Tail: Section of oak-turkey wing quill.
Body: Gold tinsel or Candlelite.
Wing: A spray of natural squirrel-tail flanked by a section of oak-turkey feather.
Shoulder: Natural deerhair spun on to the hook in front of the wings and clipped to shape.
Head: Tie-off not visible, but use a blob of clear varnish at root.

7 Badger Matuka

The Badger Matuka has been a favourite lure of mine for many years. It was invented by Hertfordshire fly-fisher Steve Stephens and is a reliable pattern, catching the better trout at most reservoirs I have fished. It swims nice and straight and imitates fry quite well. Using it from a boat on a lead-impregnated line can bring good results with brown trout.

Hook: Size 6, 8 or 10 long-shank bronze.
Tying silk: Black.
Body: White chenille ribbed with silver wire.
Thorax: A short segment of orange wool or chenille tied in behind the head.
Hackle: Hot-orange cock hackle-fibres. Throat only.
Wing: Matuka style. Two or three pairs of well-marked badger hen hackles matched dull side to dull side. Leave their tips protruding as the tail.
Head: Black varnish.

8 Missionary

Although the Missionary is an old New Zealand pattern, the modern version, created by Dick Shrive, has been used with great success since the late 1950s. The idea is to imitate a small fry, be it roach, rudd or bream, and it does this really well. It can be fished with confidence when trout (especially browns) come into the margins to gorge on fry in the latter part of the season.

Hook: Size 10, 8 or 6 Mustad long-shank bronze.
Tying silk: Black or white.
Tail: Scarlet cock hackle-fibres.
Body: White chenille ribbed with silver tinsel.
Hackle: Scarlet cock hackle-fibres. Throat only.
Wing: Teal or silver mallard breast feather tied concave to give a parachute action on sinking.
Head: Black varnish with black tying silk. Clear varnish with white.

Fish-imitating Lures 2

This is another set of proven patterns dating from the 1970s. I must choose my Appetiser lure as my favourite, because it has caught so many big fish for me and some even larger for some of my friends. It has also taken some of my best heavy-weight bags, and I have seen many reports in the angling press of it doing the same for others. The rest of the selection are useful too, even that other old-timer, Tom Ivens' Jersey Herd, is still regularly catching fish.

1 Polystickle

COMMENT

This is one of the most famous fish-imitating lure patterns. It was invented by Dick Walker in 1966 to coincide with the opening of Grafham. At that time Grafham's margins were alive with sticklebacks, and Dick's new lure was certainly most effective at tempting a lot of big fish into making a mistake. I still use the pattern from time to time and it scores as well as ever, especially when fry are about.

DRESSING

Hook: Almost any size bronze.
Tying silk: Black.
Back and tail: A strip of brown or green Raffene tied in at the bend.
Body: Underbody, silver tinsel or white Baby Doll wool, with a red or orange flash at the head. Cover with clear polythene and build it into a fish-shaped body.
Hackle: Hot-orange hackle-fibres. Throat only.
Head: Build up with silk and varnish black.

2 Roach Fry

COMMENT

This pattern was devised by David Train for use at Chew Valley Lake in late summer and autumn. It scored well for him and his friends on many occasions when they were bank fishing close to Woodford Lodge. This is always a good fry-holding area, and good-sized fish come in to feed on them, especially during the early morning. Use the Roach fry alone on a floating or sinking line according to the trout's behaviour.

DRESSING

Hook: Size 6, 8 or 10 long-shank bronze.
Tail: None.
Body: Silver tinsel ribbed with gold oval thread.
Throat hackle: White cock fibres.
Wing: This is in three layers – a spray of white goat-hair, topped by a spray of blue goat-hair, and finally a spray of black goat-hair or squirrel-tail hair.
Head: Black Varnish.

1 Polystickle　**2** Roach Fry　**3** White Marabou Lure　**4** Orange Mylar Stickle
5 Black Ghost　**6** Grey Ghost　**7** Jersey Herd　**8** Appetiser

3   White Marabou Lure

White marabou was so successful when it was
first used in my Appetiser lure that it inspired the
creation of a number of other patterns using it.
One of them was this White Marabou Lure,
which is used as a general lure pattern and
works best on a sinking line.

DRESSING

Hook: Size 10, 8 or 6 long-shank.
Tying silk: Black.
Body: Silver tinsel.
Hackle: Bright red.
Wing: White marabou with a few strands of
peacock herl worked in.
Head: Black Varnish.

4   Orange Mylar Stickle

COMMENT

This lure really does look like a stickleback or
small yearling coarse-fish fry. Some very large
trout have been caught on it and similar
patterns. Syd Brock had a 10lb brownie from
Farmoor I Reservoir in Oxfordshire while fishing
deep with a sinking shooting-head. He was
casting to a draw-off valve tower where many
small fish congregated. As the lure sank to the
bottom it must have looked like a dying, ailing
fry, because the trout took on the drop.

DRESSING

Hook: Size 10, 8 or 6 long-shank.
Tying silk: Black.
Tail and back: Brown Raffene.
Body: Silver Mylar.
Hackle: Orange.
Head: Black varnish.

5   Black Ghost

COMMENT

This is a popular lure on the reservoirs, where it
is known as a most effective pattern. It is fished
mostly on a sinking line – fast-sinker during early
season and a medium- or slow-sinker in late
spring and summer fishing. One of its strong
points is its high visibility. It shows up really well
in peaty or mud-stained water.

DRESSING

Hook: Size 10, 8 or 6 long-shank.
Tying silk: Black.
Tail: Golden-pheasant crest.
Body: Black floss or wool ribbed with silver
tinsel.
Hackle: Yellow cock.
Wing: Four white selected cock hackles.
Shoulders (optional): Jungle cock
substitute.
Head: Black varnish.

6   Grey Ghost

COMMENT

This general fancy pattern has been around for some time. It possibly imitates a small fish, and I certainly feel that it triggers a trout's aggressive instincts and that is why they take it. A sinking fly-line would be my choice when using this lure.

DRESSING

Hook: Size 10, 8 or 6 long-shank.
Tying silk: Black.
Body: Orange/red floss ribbed with silver tinsel.
Wing: Four medium blue-dun cock hackles topped by ten strands of bronze peacock herl.
Cheeks: Silver-pheasant body feathers or teal.
Eyes: Jungle cock substitute.
Head: Black varnish.

7   Jersey Herd

COMMENT

One March day at Ardleigh Reservoir, I didn't hit the jackpot until, after many fly-changes, I put on Tom Ivens' Jersey Herd. It was only a small pattern – size 12 – but the fish (browns) were certainly keen to take it. A cold east wind was blowing, and I was fishing in six feet of water with a sink-tip line, yet the fish took the fly on the drop – behaviour we normally associate with summer. This pattern can be used as either a standard wet fly or a lure which imitates small fry.

DRESSING

Hook: Size 14, 12 or 10 medium-shank for wets, Size 10, 8 or 6 long-shank for lures.
Tying silk: Black.
Underbody: Any light-coloured floss.
Body: Flat gold tinsel.
Hackle: Hot-orange or yellow.
Tail and back: Bronze peacock herl.
Head: Black varnish.

8   Appetiser

COMMENT

I designed the Appetiser in 1972 especially for the big, fry-feeding trout at Grafham. It was the first time marabou was used in a wing of a modern lure in Britain. It had tremendous success at Grafham, topped by taking the heaviest bag-limit for seven years. The Queen Mother is another reservoir where I have had great results with the Appetiser. Indeed, it works well on all water and has been one of the most successful catchers of big trout. It's not only big trout that feed on fry. I have found up to 30 fry in a 1½lb rainbow from Grafham.

DRESSING

Hook: Size 10, 8 or 6 long-shank.
Tying silk: Black.
Tail: Mixed orange, green and silver mallard fibres.
Body: White chenille ribbed with silver tinsel.
Hackle: Mixed orange, green and silver mallard. Throat only.
Underwing: White marabou (generous).
Overwing: Natural grey squirrel-tail hair.
Eyes: Optional.
Head: Black varnish.

Attractor Muddlers

American angler Don Gapen could hardly have imagined that his superb original Muddler Minnow would cause such a revolution in English reservoir fly-fishers' techniques. The Muddler Minnow craze began just after Grafham opened in 1966. It started with the standard pattern, but Mick Nicholls and I soon developed black and white versions. Then it was realised that orange killed in hot weather, and so it went on. Since then the Muddler family — some of the best are in this collection — have proved deadly catchers of rainbow in high summer. The method is to strip the lure on the surface, and although it is hard work, it produces some really exciting visual sport as the bow wave following the lure turns into a vicious pull.

1 Black Muddler

COMMENT

Some years ago I discovered a deadly method of fishing a size 12 black-bodied Muddler on the point, with two Buzzer Nymphs as droppers. The Muddler was sprayed with dry-fly silicone to make it float. Then I de-greased the rest of the leader to ensure that this would sink just below the surface film. After casting out across the wind, I allowed the flies to drift round naturally while I took up any excess slack. The Muddler acted as a controller, but was sometimes taken. The takes came mostly on the well-presented buzzers.

DRESSING

Hook: Size 12,10, 8 or 6 long-shank.
Tying silk: Black.
Body: Black floss ribbed with silver oval tinsel. Alternatively, gold tinsel ribbed with gold wire.
Wing: Black squirrel-tail hair or bucktail.
Head: Natural deerhair or deerhair dyed black.

2 Texas Rose Muddler

COMMENT

This variation of the Muddler, devised by Richard Walker, received much favour from anglers fishing at Grafham and Hanningfield reservoirs. An orange streak moving quickly across the surface really sorts out the rainbows at these large reservoirs — and that is the clue as to how this pattern should be used.

DRESSING

Hook: Size 10, 8 or 6 long-shank.
Tying silk: Black.
Body: Orange floss ribbed with silver oval tinsel.
Wing: Yellow bucktail hair.
Head: Natural deerhair.

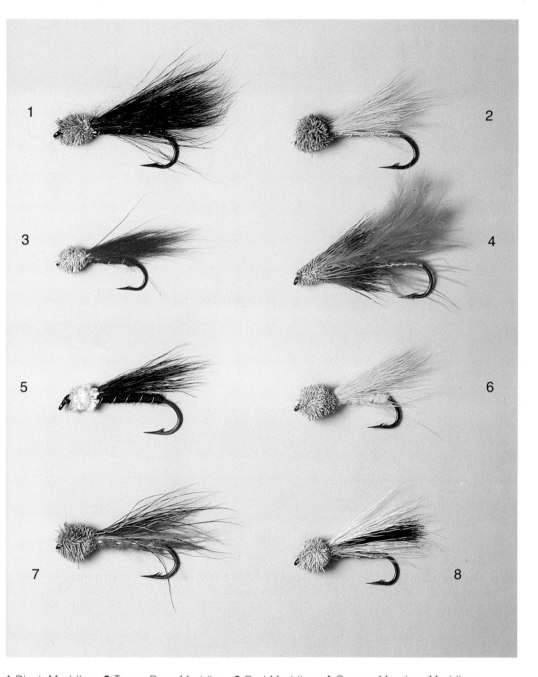

1 Black Muddler   2 Texas Rose Muddler   3 Red Muddler   4 Orange Marabou Muddler
5 Minstrel Muddler   6 Yellow Muddler   7 Rainbow Muddler   8 Badger Muddler

3 Red Muddler

COMMENT

Red works well with rainbow trout at certain times, and it is on the reservoirs and larger gravel-pits that the Red Muddler scores best, largely during summer and autumn. The clipping of any Muddler head is important. Clip to leave a large ball-shaped head for surface 'wake' fishing. Clip to a cone-shape for sunken fishing, as this gives less buoyancy.

DRESSING

Hook: Size 10, 8 or 6 long-shank.
Tying silk: Black.
Body: Red floss or wool ribbed with silver tinsel.
Wing: Red bucktail.
Head: Natural deerhair.

4 Orange Marabou Muddle

COMMENT

This is one of the most effective of the hot-weather lures. Cast it on a floating line as far downwind as you can, then strip it back as fast as possible. It is hard work, but the technique arouses fish to follow. Not all follows become takes, but enough fish will grab the lure to satisfy you. As long as a wave is on, try this lure and method when all else fails during a warm spell.

DRESSING

Hook: Size 10, 8 or 6 long-shank.
Tying silk: Black.
Body: Gold tinsel ribbed with gold wire.
Wing: Hot-orange marabou.
Head: Natural deerhair.

5 Minstrel Muddler

COMMENT

It was my good friend David Allen, from Essex, who devised this pattern. In the mid-1970s David used to invite me to fish at Hanningfield, and we had some great catches of larger-than-average trout. David's lure worked impressively at Hanningfield, but it travelled well and was later found to kill both brown and rainbow trout at all waters where it was tried. The best results came to sinking-line tactics.

DRESSING

Hook: Size 10, 8 or 6 long-shank.
Tying silk: Black.
Body: Black wool ribbed with silver oval tinsel.
Wing: Black squirrel-tail hair.
Head: Fluorescent white chenille tied ball-shaped as in the deerhair patterns.

6 Yellow Muddler

COMMENT

Yellow is completely underrated by most fly-fishers. It is easily seen when the water is murky following a big wind, and this high visibility certainly helps to attract trout. A good time to use a size 10 Yellow Muddler is during or following the Mayfly season. I have taken some good fish from the Gloucestershire gravel-pits with it, and even from Lough Mask. On one occasion John Wilshaw and I took quick limits at Church Hill Farm's large lake when mayflies were hatching – but the only artificial to bring a take was the Yellow Muddler.

DRESSING

Hook: Size 10, 8 or 6 long-shank.
Tying silk: Black.
Body: Fluorescent yellow wool ribbed with oval silver tinsel.
Wing: Yellow bucktail goat-hair.
Head: Natural deerhair.

7 Rainbow Muddler

COMMENT

The coloration of this Muddler gives the effect of a small rainbow parr. There is no logical reason for imitating a fingerling rainbow, because it is rare for natural breeding to occur in British stillwaters. However, someone thought of the idea and so created a very good attractor pattern which, fished fast across the top, catches the large rainbows whose young it represents.

DRESSING

Hook: Size 10, 8 or 6 long-shank.
Tying silk: Black.
Tail: Pink hackle-fibres.
Body: Pink wool ribbed with silver oval tinsel.
Wing: Mixed green, pink and black bucktail.
Head: Natural deerhair, clipped ball-shaped

8 Badger Muddler

COMMENT

Badger-hackle feather lures and flies are well known as effective trout-catchers. The idea behind this Muddler dressing was to create a similar lure with hair as a wing instead of feather. The more rigid hair from bucktail ensures that it does not wrap round the hook-bend when long casts are made. This would sometimes happen if badger-hackles were used. The idea can be used with other lures.

DRESSING

Hook: Size 10, 8 or 6 long-shank.
Tying silk: Black.
Body: Dark blood-red floss ribbed with silver oval tinsel.
Wing: White and black bucktail to give badger effect.
Head: Natural deerhair.

Black Lure Killers

Black is beautiful, for lures of this base colour probably consistently catch more trout than any others in the course of a season. You can have great faith in any of this selection from the earliest days of spring right through to the end of October. If the trout are sulking deep-down, use these lures on a fast-sink line. If the fish move to mid-water, use a medium sinker; and when at last the fish show on top, use a floater. Black lures will take fish in all these circumstances; no other colour has such a wide use.

1   Ace of Spades

COMMENT

The Ace of Spades, devised by Dave Collyer a few years ago, is one of the best of this set of drab lures. It has worked well for me on reservoirs, gravel-pits and small fisheries. I prefer to fish it slow and deep. Its Matuka-style dressing makes it swim very evenly on the retrieve.

DRESSING

Hook: Size 10, 8 or 6 long-shank bronze.
Tying silk: Black.
Body: Black chenille ribbed with oval tinsel.
Hackle: Guinea-fowl fibres tied in at the throat only.
Wings: Two hackles dyed black, positioned back-to-back and topped with a spray of bronze mallard.

2   Poly Butcher

COMMENT

The small wet-fly patterns, Butcher and Bloody Butcher, are excellent flies, but I wanted to extend their catching qualities and create a modern lure, for which I felt there was a need. I am happy with my creation, for although it has received little publicity, it is a pattern I often use and one with which I do well. I have had some good bags from Grafham during midsummer while using it on a slow-sinking line. Rainbows cruising at mid-water and feeding on daphnia took the lure confidently.

DRESSING

Hook: Size 10, 8 or 6 long-shank.
Tying silk: Black.
Tail: Bright red cock hackle-fibres.
Underbody: Red floss or wool.
Overbody: Stretched clear polythene strip.
Hackle: Bright red cock or black.
Wing: Squirrel-tail dyed black.
Head: Black varnish.

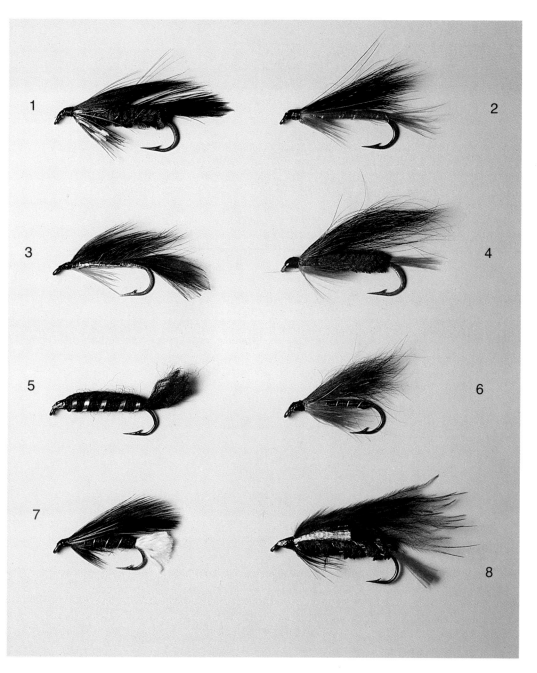

1 Ace of Spades **2** Poly Butcher **3** Black and Silver Matuka
4 Black and Orange Hairwing **5** Undertaker **6** Sweeney Todd **7** Viva
8 Christmas Tree Lure

3 Black and Silver Matuka

COMMENT

This New Zealand style of dressing makes a lure always swim on an even keel when it is being retrieved, and black and silver have always been a deadly combination in the smaller wet-fly patterns. It was to be expected, therefore, that a lure with similar characteristics would catch trout. Fish this lure by itself for the best results.

DRESSING

Hook: Size 10, 8 or 6.
Tying silk: Black.
Tail and wing: Four black cock hackles.
Body: Silver tinsel ribbed with silver wire.
Hackle: Blue.
Head: Black varnish.

4 Black and Orange Hairwing

COMMENT

This lure was given to me by Brian Gent, who specialised in fishing the London reservoirs. Brian told me he had better results with this lure from the Walthamstow and Queen Mother Reservoirs than he had with the famous Sweeney Todd.

DRESSING

Hook: Size 10, 8 or 6 long-shank.
Tying silk: Black.
Tail: Orange hackle-fibres.
Body: Black chenille ribbed with silver wire.
Hackle: Orange. Throat only.
Wing: Black squirrel-tail hair.
Head: Black varnish.

5 Undertaker

COMMENT

I was introduced to this fly by a Draycote Reservoir fly-fisher, who had been getting some good catches of brown trout with it while fishing there with bottom-searching methods. It is a pattern well worth having in your box, especially if the water you fish holds a fair stock of browns.

DRESSING

Hook: Size 10, 8 or 6 long-shank.
Tying silk: Black.
Tail and body: Black wool. Tie as for Baby Doll, but add wide silver tinsel ribbing to the body.
Head: Black varnish.

6 Sweeney Todd

COMMENT

This famous Dick Walker pattern has stood the test of time. Dick transferred the known attractor qualities of a red tail to the throat region in an effort to reduce short takes – an idea which certainly proved successful.

DRESSING

Hook: Size 10, 8 or 6 long-shank bronze.
Tying silk: Black.
Tail: None.
Body: Black floss ribbed with fine silver tinsel.
Throat: Three turns of magenta fluorescent wool.
Hackle: Magenta cock fibres. Beard only.
Wing: Squirrel-tail hair dyed black.
Head: Black varnish.

7 Viva

COMMENT

The Viva is really an extension of my Black Chenille lure. However, that little blob of green is definitely an extra ingredient that the trout like. I rate this pattern very highly, and it is one of my favourites. I use it both as a lure and as a wet fly, and my results have been excellent. I have used it with sunken and floating-line tactics and through a whole season, from March until the end of October.

DRESSING

Hook: Size 12, 10, 8 or 6 ordinary and long-shank.
Tying silk: Black.
Tail: Fluorescent green wool.
Body: Black chenille ribbed with silver tinsel.
Hackle: Black cock with the optional addition of more green in a fluorescent green hackle.
Wing: Four black cock hackles. Some tyers use black squirrel hair; others, black marabou.
Head: Black varnish.

8 Christmas Tree Lure

COMMENT

This lure has become popular over the past three seasons. It has accounted for many big brown trout from Rutland, so it has earned a good reputation. It works well on most waters, especially when fished slow and deep early in the season.

DRESSING

Hook: Size 10, 8 or 6 long-shank bronze.
Tying silk: Black.
Tail: Spray of fluorescent lime-green floss silk.
Body: Black chenille ribbed with gold oval thread.
Hackle: Fluorescent pink floss silk.
Wing: Spray of black marabou feather.
Head: Black varnish.

Dog Nobblers

Love them or hate them, you cannot ignore these controversial dressings. The basic pattern was devised by Trevor Housby, from Lymington, Hampshire. This set covers the eight main colours which have produced good catches.

1 Orange Dog Nobbler

COMMENT

Although most orange lures are fished fast on or close to the surface, this one works well fished deep with long, steady pulls. The Orange Nobbler will kill early in the season as long as it is fished close to the bottom.

DRESSING

Hook: Size 8 long-shank.
Tying silk: Black with lead-wire underbody at head.
Tail: Hot-orange marabou.
Body: Hot-orange chenille ribbed with gold wire.
Head: Bornze peacock herl.
Head finish: Black varnish.

2 Olive Dog Nobbler

COMMENT

The Olive Nobbler is a good imitation of a swimming damselfly nymph on its way to the bank or a reed-bed to hatch out, a frequent occurrence during high summer. Try this pattern at that time, fishing it on a floating line and retrieving it with rapid, short, sharp jerks.

DRESSING

Hook: Size 8 long-shank.
Tying silk: Black with lightly-leaded head section.
Tail: Olive marabou.
Body: Olive chenille ribbed with copper wire.
Head: Bronze peacock herl.
Head finish: Black varnish.

1 Orange **2** Olive **3** White **4** Brown
5 Black **6** Pink **7** Fluorescent Green **8** Yellow

3 White Dog Nobbler

COMMENT

This is a fry-imitating lure. John Wilshaw, former Editor of *Trout and Salmon* magazine, had three tremendous catches of big trout from Rutland's North Arm shallows while trying the pattern in its early days. John and his boat partner were drifting slowly, using the rudder to keep the boat bow-first downwind. The tactic was for each man to side-cast with a floating line. The retrieve was such as to fish the lure sink-and-draw. John tried several other fry-imitating lures during the three sessions, but none was anywhere near as successful.

DRESSING

Hook: Size 10, 8 or 6 long-shank.
Tying silk: Black with lead-wire underbody at head.
Tail: White marabou.
Body: White chenille ribbed with silver oval thread.
Head: Bronze peacock herl.
Head finish: Black varnish.

4 Brown Dog Nobbler

COMMENT

The Brown Nobbler should be fished deep. If you can make the lure 'crawl' along the bottom, it imitates a large leech or larva. Brown is a good colour to use early in the season from the bank. Later, try it in deep water from a boat. Always fish this pattern on a sinking line.

DRESSING

Hook: Size 8 long-shank.
Tying silk: Black with leaded underbody at head.
Tail: Brown marabou.
Body: Brown chenille ribbed with copper wire.
Head: Bronze peacock herl.
Head finish: Black varnish.

5 Black Dog Nobbler

COMMENT

This style of dressing has given the basic Black Lure a new action in the sink-and-draw movement achieved by retrieving in jerks. Early-season fishing off the bank with a size 10 Black Nobbler at Foremark proved so deadly that in a morning's fishing I caught 35 browns and a rainbow. Most were over 2lb and I shook them off, but other anglers were struggling to get a fish. The secret was the small Black Nobbler and long casts (40yds) with a medium-sink shooting-head.

DRESSING

Hook: Size 10, 8 or 6 weighted at head with lead.
Tying silk: Black.
Tail: Generous plume of long-fibred black marabou.
Body: Black chenille ribbed with silver oval thread.
Thorax: Peacock herl.
Head: Black varnish.

6 Pink Dog Nobbler

COMMENT

Nobblers were as yet unheard of when an angler at Walthamstow showed me a shocking-pink lure with which he had been catching fish. It was the same as a Nobbler, but without the weighted head. I first tried it after a morning's hard fishing at Church Hill Farm without a fish. On it went and soon out came a four rainbow limit-bag. It worked similarly at Farmoor II on a hard day. However, although it was good, once the news about pink had spread and others began to use it, it became much less effective.

DRESSING

Hook: Size 10, 8 or 6 long-shank.
Tying silk: Black with lead wire beneath the dressing at the head.
Tail: Shocking-pink marabou.
Body: Shocking-pink chenille ribbed with silver tinsel.
Head: Bronze peacock herl.
Head finish: Black varnish.

7 Fluorescent Green Dog Nobbler

COMMENT

I had a terrific catch early in the 1985 season while using this lure at Packington. I set up with a medium-sinking line and used a 4-metre leader. 2 metres from the point, where I had the Green Nobbler, I tied on a size 10 unweighted Viva as dropper. The Nobbler bounced along the lake-bed on the retrieve. I caught two-thirds of a good morning's catch on the Nobbler and the rest on the Viva. The Nobbler acted as a controller and the Viva fished a few feet off the bottom, so I caught fish in mid-water as well as those bottom-sulkers.

DRESSING

Hook: Size 8 long-shank.
Tying silk: Black with lead-wire underbody at head.
Tail: Green marabou.
Body: Fluorescent green chenille ribbed with silver oval thread.
Head: Bronze peacock herl.
Head finish: Black varnish.

8 Yellow Dog Nobbler

COMMENT

What a lure this has proved! I caught a heavy all-brown limit on it at Tittesworth with shooting-head, sinking-line tactics when all other lures failed. Then there was the memorable occasion at Avington. A double-figure fish had refused all offerings, but then I remembered the Yellow Nobbler from that Tittesworth day. On it went. That trout changed from a docile, lazy fish to one of fin-bristling savagery as it raced across the pool to hammer my fly. The result was a seemingly uncatchable 11½lb rainbow on the bank.

DRESSING

Hook: Size 10, 8 or 6.
Tying silk: Black with lead wire beneath dressing at head.
Tail: Yellow marabou.
Body: Yellow chenille ribbed with silver oval thread.
Head: Bronze peacock herl.
Head finish: Black varnish.

Frog Nobblers

I first tied this pattern in White and Silver and Black and Gold on size 12 hooks for the French Open Stillwater Trout Championships in 1982.

John Wilshaw named the fly (with apologies to our French friends) and won the event, catching quite a few trout on the White and Silver.

1   Pink and Silver Frog Nobbler

COMMENT

The lead-foil specified in all these dressings comes from the tops of wine or brandy bottles. It is cut into thin strips, whipped on to the hook-shank and then secured tightly so that it will not slip about beneath the body dressing. This pink version is purely for shock tactics. The trout either attack it every time you cast, or they are terrified and leave the area!

DRESSING

Hook: Size 12, 10 or 8 weighted with lead-foil.
Tying silk: Black.
Tail: Fluorescent pink marabou.
Body: Silver Mylar tube.
Head: Black varnish.

2   Black and Gold Frog Nobbler

COMMENT

Frog Nobblers – which come in many colours – are all tied on size 12 or 10 hooks and are weighted to give a sink-and-draw action similar to the Dog Nobblers. The Black and Gold works particularly well in gin-clear waters.

DRESSING

Hook: Size 12 or 10 normal or long-shank.
Tying silk: Black.
Tail: Generous spray of fine-tipped black marabou with a little gold Flashabou.
Body: Underbody of floss over which a sleeve of gold Mylar tube is slid.
Hackle: Hot-orange.
Head: Black varnish with eyes painted on.

1 Pink and Silver **2** Black and Gold **3** Olive and Gold **4** Yellow and Gold
5 White and Silver **6** Red White and Silver **7** Orange and Gold **8** Blue and Silver

3   Olive and Gold Frog Nobbler

COMMENT

This version is at its best when the damselflies are active, from midsummer through to September. It pays to tie a few unweighted, so that they can be fished across the surface at the appropriate time. The 'wiggly' action of the tail is similar to the swimming action of the damselfly nymph, and the gold body obviously adds to the attraction.

DRESSING

Hook: Size 12, 10 or 8 weighted with lead-foil.
Tying silk: Black.
Tail: Olive marabou.
Body: Gold Mylar tube.
Head: Black varnish.

4   Yellow and Gold Frog Nobbler

COMMENT

This pattern has proved that fluorescent yellow is far more effective than ordinary bright yellow. It cannot fail to be seen by the trout in the immediate vicinity. It has caught me many trout on both floating and sinking lines and from both small fisheries and large reservoirs.

DRESSING

Hook: Size 12, 10 or 8 weighted with lead-foil.
Tying silk: Black.
Tail: Fluorescent yellow marabou.
Body: Gold Mylar tube.
Hackle: Orange cock.
Head: Black varnish with eyes painted on.

5 . White and Silver Frog Nobbler

COMMENT

This colour combination, along with black, was devised for use in the French National Stillwater Trout Championships in 1982. I thought it worth trying a more delicate type of weighted fly rather than the larger Dog Nobbler. The venue was of gravel-pit type with quite clear water. Four of us caught about sixty trout, both browns and rainbows, all of which were returned. One fine rainbow of over 5lb regurgitated some sticklebacks as I returned it.

DRESSING

Hook: Size 12, 10 or 8 weighted with lead-foil.
Tying silk: Black.
Tail: White marabou.
Body: Silver Mylar tube.
Head: Black varnish.

6 Red, White and Silver Frog Nobbler

COMMENT

I took a great catch of rainbows from Martin Pollard's Churn Pool in Gloucestershire on this pattern. The best part of it was that I didn't try the pattern until early afternoon, after trying several others, and at that time I hadn't caught a fish. We have to accept that trout do prefer different presentations of the fly, nymph or lure on different days.

DRESSING

Hook: Size 12, 10 or 8 weighted with lead-foil.
Tying silk: Black.
Tail: Equal amounts of red and white marabou.
Body: Silver Mylar tube.
Head: Black varnish.

7 Orange and Gold Frog Nobbler

COMMENT

Orange lures are normally reserved for high-summer conditions, but this delicate pattern can be used on size 12 hooks with great effect throughout the season. Try one when you are next fishing a small clear-water fishery. Use a floating line and allow the lure to sink well down before retrieving it in short sharp twitches. Sometimes I twitch the rod-top as well, which makes the lure jig about tantalisingly.

DRESSING

Hook: Size 12, 10 or 8 weighted with lead-foil.
Tying silk: Black.
Tail: Orange marabou.
Body: Gold Mylar tube.
Head: Black varnish.

8 Blue and Silver Frog Nobbler

COMMENT

This dressing is a little fancy, but you can add or subtract any material from any pattern. That is the fun of tying your own flies. Blue is an unusual colour for this type of lure, and it always brings a wry smile from Bedford International fly-fishers Bob Morey and Brian Leadbetter. But even they have to concede when we are fishing an old lake-type of fishery such as Patshull Park. This lure is well worth trying on waters which have been hammered. It catches a lot of fish.

DRESSING

Hook: Size 12, 10 or 8 weighted with lead-foil.
Tying silk: Black.
Body: Silver Mylar tube.
Hackle: Black cock.
Head: Black varnish with eyes painted on.

High-summer Lures

These are patterns to use towards the end of June on reservoirs stocked with rainbow trout. The method is nearly always to fish fast, close to the surface. It was Albert Whillock's hot-orange Whisky Fly that started the orange craze. I met Albert regularly at Grafham. Although elderly, he was a fine caster and known for his 'sweet style', as it all looked so good when he was demonstrating. When into his seventies, Albert broke his forearm while punching for distance, but he soon healed and the injury never slowed him down afterwards.

1 Mickey Finn

COMMENT

The Mickey Finn lure, or streamer fly, as the Americans call it, is deadly for summer rainbows on both sides of the Atlantic. I have scored well at Grafham in hot weather by stripping a Mickey Finn fast across the surface. The gaudy flash of colour seems to bring out the killer instinct in rainbows. They smash into the lure, giving a solid take, and seldom come off in the fight. If the weather is hot and not much is doing, use a Mickey Finn.

DRESSING

Hook: Size 6, 8 or 10 long-shank bronze or nickel.
Tying silk: Black.
Body: Silver tinsel ribbed with silver wire.
Wing: Red and yellow goat-hair or bucktail evenly mixed. Other hair, such as skunk or dyed squirrel-tail, will do.
Head: Black varnish.

2 Phosphorescent Scale Fry

COMMENT

This lure uses some of the new materials which are rated so highly. The overall effect gives the illusion of an 'extra-visible' fish, and the lure is luminous when fished in the deepest, darkest water. It proved it could catch both rainbows and browns during experiments in the 1985 season. I'm sure we shall be hearing much more of it.

DRESSING

Hook: Size 8 or 6 long-shank.
Tying silk: Black.
Tail: Fluorescent green wool or floss.
Body: Pearl Mylar tube.
Hackle: Hot-orange cock.
Wing: White marabou with a spray of phosphorescent green Flashabou on top.
Head: Black varnish.

1 Mickey Finn   **2** Phosphorescent Scale Fry   **3** Leprechaun   **4** Whisky Fly
5 Orange and Gold Streamer   **6** Dunkeld Lure   **7** Breathaliser   **8** Orange Chenille Lure

3   Leprechaun

COMMENT

It is not unusual in June, July and August for a reservoir to be green with algae. Several years ago, Pete Wood discovered that Grafham rainbows would go mad for fluorescent lime-green during this period. On his first attempt with the lure he caught his limit-bag within an hour, whilst everyone else remained fishless. The Leprechaun has proved just as effective many times since then. It is one of those patterns that either 'murders' fish or fails to attract a take at all. The same tying style in black, orange, white and yellow completes a useful set.

DRESSING

Hook: Size 6, 8 or 10 long-shank bronze.
Tying silk: Black.
Tail: Green hackle-fibres.
Body: Fluorescent lime-green chenille ribbed with silver tinsel.
Hackle: Green hackle-fibres. Beard only.
Wing: Four selected green hackles.
Head: Black varnish.

4   Whisky Fly

COMMENT

This pattern was devised by Albert Willock, veteran fly-fisher and expert caster, for catching rainbows at Hanningfield and Grafham. The history of bright orange lures begins with this pattern, which came into prominence in the early 1970s. It is now established as an excellent catcher of rainbows.

DRESSING

Hook: Size 10, 8 or 6 long-shank.
Tying silk: Red.
Tail: Orange cock hackle-fibres.
Body: Red floss ribbed with gold tinsel.
Hackle: Hot-orange cock.
Wing: Orange bucktail or goat-hair.
Head: Red varnish.

5   Orange and Gold Streamer

COMMENT

This is another lively member of the orange lure family. The pulsating fibres of the marabou underwing are controlled to some extent by the hair overwing. With a steady retrieve, the combination gives a shimmering effect that attracts trout. It is mostly a rainbow pattern and it fishes well on floating or sinking lines.

DRESSING

Hook: Size 10, 8 or 6 long-shank.
Tying silk: Black.
Tail: Orange cock hackle-fibres.
Body: Gold tinsel ribbed with gold wire.
Hackle: Orange cock.
Underwing: Orange marabou.
Overwing: Squirrel-tail hair dyed orange.
Head: Black varnish.

6 Dunkeld Lure

COMMENT

Black Lures and Dunkeld Lures were favoured by the comparatively few anglers who fished when Grafham opened in 1966. Richard Walker used this lure a lot, and it was deadly with the big rainbows present in Grafham in those early days. The lure still works well today.

DRESSING

Hook: Size 10, 8 or 6 long-shank.
Tying silk: Black.
Tail: Yellow cock hackle-fibres.
Body: Gold tinsel ribbed with gold wire.
Body hackle: Palmered hot-orange cock.
Wing: Bronze mallard.
Head: Black varnish.

7 Breathaliser

COMMENT

Chew Valley fly-fisher Alec Iles devised this lure to imitate a stickleback. It accounted for many fine limit-bags, with the best results when it was fished with a fast retrieve.

DRESSING

Hook: Size 10, 8 or 6 long-shank.
Tying silk: Black.
Tail: Black cock hackle-fibres.
Body: Silver tinsel.
Wings: Two orange cock hackles with a pair of green hackles of similar length, one on either side.
Hackle: Badger hen wound full circle.
Eyes: Jungle cock or substitute.
Head: Black varnish.

8 Orange Chenille Lure

COMMENT

This lure was a natural follow-on to the black version, and the water at which it worked really well was Grafham. In the mid-1970s huge daphnia blooms spread across Grafham during the summer and at times the rainbows were feeding exclusively on daphnia. The blooms rise and fall in the water with variations in the light. On bright days they are well down; on dull days, close to the surface. Daphnia-feeding rainbows love orange lures, and on bright days an Orange Chenille fished mid-water on a medium-sinking line is an excellent method.

DRESSING

Hook: Size 10, 8 or 6 long-shank.
Tying silk: Black.
Tail: Hot-orange hackle-fibres.
Body: Orange chenille ribbed with gold tinsel.
Hackle: Hot-orange.
Wing: Four selected hot-orange cock hackles.
Head: Black varnish.

Drab Lures

This is another selection of sober black lures which always give a good account of themselves when fished slow and deep. Geoffrey Bucknall's Beastie was a forerunner of the lead-headed patterns we use today. Geoffrey always says that he can't understand why such a fuss is made of the Dog Nobbler, while his Beastie is very similar, but the name just didn't catch on. The Wormfly is an old pattern which still has a good reputation, while the fantastic results of the Black Chenille speak for themselves. However, patterns such as the Red Devil are little known, although this one is regarded as the primary killing lure by many good anglers at Eyebrook and elsewhere.

1 Black Marabou Lure

COMMENT

This is an easy-to-tie variation of the old Black Lure which has proved itself over the years. It becomes a slim, streamlined lure when wet. It is good for early-season bank-fishing when fished on a medium- to fast-sinking line.

DRESSING

Hook: Size 10, 8 or 6 long-shank.
Tying silk: Black.
Body: Silver tinsel.
Underwing: Black marabou.
Overwing: A few strands of bronze peacock herl.
Head: Black varnish.

2 Black Chenille Lure

COMMENT

What an incredible pattern this has proved! I devised it for the elusive Draycote brown trout in the reservoir's second season. Trout were feeding in deep water on caddis grubs that had built protective outer cases of black rotted straw. The Black Chenille fished on a fast-sinking lead-core line was an overnight hit. A new era had begun with chenille as a body material and lead-core trolling line substituted for the traditional fly-line. The combination has accounted for thousands of big trout in the past fifteen years.

DRESSING

Hook: Size 10, 8 or 6 long-shank.
Tying silk: Black.
Tail: Black cock hackle-fibres.
Body: Black chenille ribbed with silver tinsel.
Hackle: Black cock.
Wings: Four selected black cock hackles.
Head: Black varnish.

1 Black Marabou Lure **2** Black Chenille Lure **3** Blue and Black Hairwing
4 Skunk **5** Red Devil **6** Green Sweeney **7** Wormfly **8** Beastie

3 Blue and Black Hairwing

COMMENT

No matter what comments I get from my fishing mates, I am now a fan of the colour blue in a fly or lure. This lure has only a tiny portion of blue mixed with the deadly black base, but it catches its share of trout. It is a good general-purpose pattern for trout and sea trout.

DRESSING

Hook: Size 10, 8 or 6 long-shank.
Tying silk: Black.
Body: Black floss ribbed with silver tinsel.
Hackle: Kingfisher-blue cock.
Wing: Black squirrel-tail hair.
Head: Black varnish.

4 Skunk

COMMENT

This is an American pattern which was given to me by Nick Nicholson to try on Pitsford reservoir. As might be expected from this colour combination, it caught me a few fish. However, I have not used it often.

DRESSING

Hook: Size 10, 8 or 6.
Tying silk: Black.
Tail: Yellow hackle-fibres.
Body: Black chenille.
Hackle: Long-fibred brown hen, fully circular.
Wing: White bucktail.
Head: Black varnish.

5 Red Devil

COMMENT

The matuka-style tying of a lure came to my notice in the early 1970s. Kettering tackle-dealer Norman Spring gave me a matuka-tied fly to try at Eyebrook, where he said the pattern was catching well for his customers. Norman was known to tell a good tale, but on this occasion he was spot on. The lure remains a true favourite with Eyebrook regulars to this day. It is excellent for browns.

DRESSING

Hook: Size 10, 8 or 6 long-shank.
Tying silk: Black.
Tail and back: Four selected black cock fibres tied matuka-style.
Body: Red chenille ribbed with gold oval thread.
Hackle: Black cock.
Head: Black varnish.

6 Green Sweeney

Having a brightly-coloured aiming point close to the head of a lure was Richard Walker's idea. Originally, in his Sweeney Todd pattern, he chose magenta as that colour, and it was a winner. This variation is also a winner. Try it as a mid-water lure in algae and daphnia blooms – the rainbows love it.

DRESSING

Hook: Size 10, 8 or 6 long-shank.
Tying silk: Black.
Body: Black floss ribbed with silver tinsel and with the last ³⁄₁₆ inch next to the eye fluorescent green floss.
Hackle: Fluorescent green.
Wing: Black squirrel-tail hair.
Head: Black varnish.

7 Wormfly

COMMENT

This is an old pattern which can also be tied on tandem hooks. It was a favourite pattern at Eyebrook, Chew Valley and Pitsford well before Grafham opened, but it worked there too. Fished slow and deep, it imitates many bottom-crawling creatures – caddis, leeches, beetles, damsel or dragonfly larvae. It has stood the test of time and is as successful today as ever it was. It works equally well with rainbows and browns.

DRESSING

Hook: Size 10, 8 or 6 long-shank.
Tying silk: Black.
Tail: Red wool.
Body: Bronze peacock herl to half-way down the hook-shank. At this half-way stage, tie in another tail-like snippet of red wool beneath the shank and a fully-circular medium-brown hen hackle. Continue the bronze peacock herl body to the eye and finally tie in another fully-circular medium-brown hen hackle.
Head: Black varnish.

8 Beastie

COMMENT

Geoffrey Bucknall developed this lure for Grafham and in his early experiments hooked many good fish as the Beastie nose-dived to the bottom. The weighted head and the long marabou plumes made this a forerunner of Trevor Housby's Dog Nobblers. This lure may appear 'messy' while dry, but once in the water, and being retrieved, it becomes almost a living creature.

DRESSING

Hook: Size 6 long-shank.
Tying silk: Black.
Body: Black floss silk ribbed with silver tinsel.
Hackle: Pinch of orange marabou.
Underwing: Long strip of orange marabou.
Main wing: Two black marabou plumes tied back-to-back.
Cheeks: Black and white barred silver-pheasant flank feathers.
Eyes: Jungle cock over the cheeks.
Head: Two layers of medium-thick lead wire.

Colourful Killers I

No lure had ever been banned without a reason being given until the Nailer Fly arrived. It just has to be good, doesn't it? Goldie is a brown trout phenomenon and a great point-fly when fished wet in sizes 12 or 10. Hamill's Killer, too, has shown good form; indeed, any lure that works on Lough Mask's wild browns has to be rather special. This little matuka-styled lure comes from New Zealand, the country from which we borrowed the dorsal-fin idea for well-known English patterns such as Dave Collyer's Ace of Spades and Steve Stephens' Badger Matuka.

1 Goldie

COMMENT

Rutland has given some fabulous brown trout fishing, but it was in the summer of 1977 while fishing there that I realised just how attractive a gold-bodied lure was to the bigger browns. I blended gold with yellow and black and came up with this pattern, which I christened the Goldie. It has been a consistent pattern at Rutland and has taken many limit-bags in both tandem and single-hook form. The best results come when it is used on a sinking line with a fairly fast retrieve.

DRESSING

Hook: Size 6, 8 or 10 long-shank bronze, single or tandem.
Tying silk: Black.
Tail: Yellow hackle-fibres.
Body: Gold tinsel ribbed with gold wire.
Hackle: Yellow hackle-fibres. Beard only.
Underwing: Yellow goat-hair or skunk hair.
Overwing: Black goat-hair or skunk hair.
Head: Black varnish.

2 Cardinal

COMMENT

This was one of the first lure patterns I used in the early 1960s, when Pitsford Reservoir opened, and it was good for both rainbow and brown trout. A size 10 hook was easily the most successful. I had good results with it at Eyebrook, too. The Cardinal is rarely spoken of as a popular pattern, but it is a very good one. Perhaps it is just old and forgotten. Try it and you'll find that trout react to it the same today as they did in the 1960s. I recommend it.

DRESSING

Hook: Size 10, 8 or 6 long-shank.
Tying silk: Red or black.
Tail: Red feather-fibre.
Body: Red chenille ribbed with silver oval tinsel.
Hackle: Bright red cock.
Wing: Four selected red cock hackles.
Head (optional): Red or black varnish.

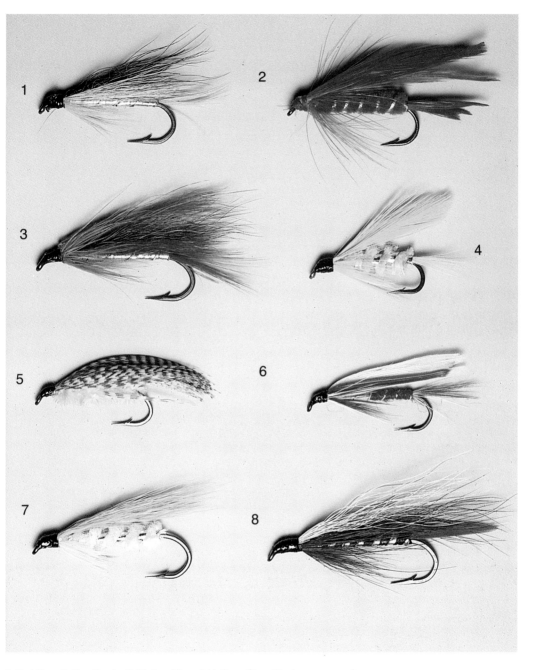

1 Goldie   2 Cardinal   3 Nailer Fly   4 Yellow Chenille Lure
5 Hamill's Killer   6 Parmachene Belle Lure   7 Mrs Palmer   8 Blue Jane

3 Nailer Fly

COMMENT

What a story lies behind this old pattern! In the 1950s Northampton angler Dick Shrive was catching more than his fair share of trout from Ravensthorpe, and a few regulars began to get jealous, as their results were poor by comparison. Dick was using the Nailer, and he told the other anglers that this was the reason for his success. He was also using a sinking line. The next week Dick arrived to find a notice pinned to the boathouse door: 'The Nailer will not be used at this water'. Yet at that stage no other fisherman had actually seen the fly!

DRESSING

Hook: Size 10, 8 or 6 long-shank.
Tying silk: Black.
Tail: Red cock hackle-fibres or red hair.
Body: Gold tinsel ribbed with gold wire.
Hackle: Chocolate-brown cock.
Underwing: Bright red hair, goat-hair or bucktail.
Overwing: Brown bucktail hair.
Head: Black varnish.

4 Yellow Chenille Lure

COMMENT

This variation of the popular chenille-bodied fly-range can be very good indeed. I remember one red-letter day at Rutland Water when, side-casting and fishing deep from a rudder-drifting boat, my partner and I had tried several patterns before I put on the Yellow Chenille. We took the boat on a drift across Old Hall Bay and when we reached the far bank I had boated four browns of more than 4lb. We each finished with a double-limit of heavier-than-average fish that May day, while most other boats did poorly.

DRESSING

Hook: Size 10, 8 or 6 long-shank.
Tying silk: Black.
Tail: Yellow hackle-fibres.
Body: Yellow chenille ribbed with silver or gold tinsel.
Hackle: Yellow cock.
Wing: Four selected yellow cock hackles.
Head: Black varnish.

5 Hamill's Killer

COMMENT

This pattern from New Zealand was given to me by Godfrey Hudson, from Devon. It has produced some good results, and in the strangest circumstances. Once, when mayfly were hatching on Ireland's Lough Mask, I was still not catching after trying all the acceptable imitations. I looked in the box for something else with yellow, and there was the untried Hamill's Killer. On it went, and straight away I started catching good brown trout. It has since proved a good general pattern as well as a mayfly standby.

DRESSING

Hook: Size 10, 8 or 6 long-shank.
Tying silk: Black.
Body: Bright yellow chenille.
Wings: This pattern has two wings of mallard feathers dyed pale yellow-grey. The first wing is half-way down the shank and should be kept short. The second wing is as normal and longer.
Hackle (optional): Black.
Head: Black varnish.

6 Parmachene Belle Lure

COMMENT

This American streamer-type of pattern has been used in this country for a long time now. It is a general pattern, and my choice of presentation is to use it as a single lure fished on a five-metre leader on a sinking line. Brian Gent describes a wet-fly version of this pattern, which he rates highly, in his guest chapter.

DRESSING

Hook: Size 10, 8 or 6.
Tying silk: Black.
Tail: Red and white hackle-fibres.
Body: Rear part, red; front half, white ribbed with gold wire.
Hackle: Red and white mixed. Throat only.
Wing: White goose feather-fibre, with a pair of slim red feather-fibre strips along each side.
Head: Black varnish.

7 Mrs Palmer

COMMENT

Richard Walker devised this pattern in about 1970. He wanted a lure that was highly visible in the churned-up coloured water of the downwind reservoir shore-line. As salmon-fishers have discovered with their Yellow-belly lures, game-fish can pick out this colour well in these conditions. But it is also a good pattern to try when the water is clear – trout sometimes like yellow very much.

DRESSING

Hook: Size 10, 8 or 6 long-shank.
Tying silk: Black.
Body: White chenille ribbed with silver tinsel.
Hackle: White cock fibres.
Wing: Yellow goat-hair or bucktail.
Head: Black varnish.

8 Blue Jane

COMMENT

This lure was given to me for trial by David Train, of Swindon. He had been doing well with it at Chew Valley and Blagdon in the West Country, but I managed to make it work on the Midlands reservoirs as well. It is not a favourite of mine, but it is a good change-pattern when the old favourites are failing.

DRESSING

Hook: Size 10, 8 or 6 long-shank.
Tying silk: Black.
Tail: Red hackle-fibres.
Body: Black floss ribbed with silver tinsel.
Hackle: Kingfisher-blue.
Underwing: Blue bucktail.
Overwing: White bucktail.
Head: Black varnish.

Colourful Killers 2

This is a mixed bunch, with the Baby Dolls prominent in their many colour changes. I am always amazed that simple pieces of wool lashed to a hook can be so deadly at catching trout, especially when, on occasions, these same fish cannot be tempted with near-perfect imitations of the fly that is actually hatching. Refer to the dressing of the Original Baby Doll in the section headed 'Fish-imitating lures 1' for details of how to tie the Baby Doll (page 64).

1 Yellow Dorothy Matuka

COMMENT

The Yellow Dorothy is a well-known New Zealand matuka pattern which is deadly for rainbows. It was recommended to me by Ian Hoyle, from North Wales, who said it had also scored well with Canadian rainbows. When water temperatures are rising quite rapidly, rainbows are prepared to chase more. I feel this lure will score on most of our British waters. Certainly it is different and looks effective.

DRESSING

Hook: Size 8 or 6 medium-shank bronze.
Tying silk: Black.
Tail: Bright red cock hackle-fibres.
Body: Yellow chenille.
Rib: Fine oval silver.
Wing: Four Plymouth Rock selected cock hackles tied in matuka-style, forming a silver rib. The matuka tail should be left long, equal to body length. This will lie above the red tail.
Hackle: A few fibres of Plymouth Rock cock. Beard only.
Head: Black varnish.

2 Fluorescent Pink Baby Doll

COMMENT

Many new patterns were created when it was realised that pink could be a deadly colour for attracting rainbows. This version of the Baby Doll was as successful as any. It must be stressed that gaudy lures such as this should be used in moderation. They can either catch you a quick limit or leave you with a blank, especially if you persist with them on the wrong day.

DRESSING

Hook: Size 10, 8 or 6 long-shank.
Tying silk: Black.
Tail and Back: Pink fluorescent wool.
Body: White fluorescent wool.
Head: Black varnish.

1 Yellow Dorothy Matuka **2** Fluorescent Pink Baby Doll **3** Fluorescent Green Baby Doll
4 Dambuster **5** Spruce **6** Fluorescent Orange Baby Doll
7 Fluorescent Red Baby Doll **8** Mallard and Silver

3 Fluorescent Green Baby Doll

COMMENT

During the past fifteen years the Baby Doll series has accounted for many thousands of trout. This pattern was one of the first variations. Fluorescent green has been used in other variation patterns, and it is recognised now as perhaps the most important additive colour. Many fly-fishers look at the colour fluorescent yellow and see it as lime-green. Watch out for this; it's a mistake easily made.

DRESSING

Hook: Size 10, 8 or 6 long-shank.
Tying silk: Black.
Tail and back: Green fluorescent wool.
Body: White fluorescent wool.
Head: Black varnish.

4 Dambuster

COMMENT

This is a Richard Walker pattern with the same characteristics as the well-known Wormfly. Dick found he caught a number of good trout on it in the vicinity of dam walls on the reservoirs. He also found that rainbow trout occasionally took this lure when it lay static on the bottom. I have found it a fairly efficient caddis imitation, to be fished slow and deep.

DRESSING

Hook: Size 10, 8 or 6 long-shank.
Tying silk: Black.
Tail: Yellow wool.
Body: Bronze peacock herl with ginger hen hackle added half-way along shank.
Hackle: Repeat ginger hackle.
Head: Black varnish.

5 Spruce

COMMENT

This is another American pattern which has a reputation for arousing rainbows' curiosity. I believe badger hackles make a perfect 'fishy' silhouette when they are used as wings, although they are feathers we tend to neglect when we are creating new patterns. The Spruce should be used as a general change-pattern.

DRESSING

Hook: Size 10, 8 or 6 long-shank.
Tying silk: Black.
Tail: Peacock herl.
Body: Red floss over rear third of hook; then bronze peacock herl.
Hackle: Badger hen.
Wing: Four selected badger cock hackles.
Head: Black varnish.

6 Fluorescent Orange Baby Doll

COMMENT

Orange seems to bring out the best in rainbows when they are close to the surface. Even if the trout are not visibly rising on dull, cloudy days, you can be sure they won't be far down. Fish this lure fast across the surface after making a long cast with a floating line. Results can be spectacular, with July and August the best months on all large reservoirs.

DRESSING

Hook: Size 10, 8 or 6 long-shank.
Tying silk: Black.
Tail and back: Orange fluorescent wool.
Body: White fluorescent wool.
Head: Black varnish.

7 Fluorescent Red Baby Doll

COMMENT

Somewhere along the line this lure was given the nickname of 'Jam Sandwich', I'll let you work that one out. It's an excellent lure to use in midsummer with a Wet-Cel II line. It tempts rainbows which are feeding on daphnia in mid-water. Watch out for takes on the drop.

DRESSING

Hook: Size 10, 8 or 6 long-shank.
Tying silk: Black.
Tail and Back: Red fluorescent wool.
Body: White fluorescent wool.
Head: Black varnish.

8 Mallard and Silver

COMMENT

This can be used as a general 'flasher' lure stripped fast on a sinking line, or it can be fished in autumn as a small coarse-fish imitation. It looks rather like a first-year roach when fished on a size 8 or 6 hook. The retrieve for fry imitation should be slow and subtle.

DRESSING

Hook: Size 10, 8 or 6.
Tying silk: Black.
Body: Silver mallard
Hackle: White cock.
Wing: Bronze mallard.
Head: Black varnish.

Puppy Lures

These carrot-shaped lures were an instant hit with anglers in the West Midlands and the news travelled fast. In 1985 they began to appear everywhere. John Golding told me they were so good that he could catch fish even better when the lure's tail had been chewed off. They certainly catch a lot of trout and are on a par with the Nobblers, but they are good at catching anglers as well. On a recent visit to Rutland the French team purchased Stuart Illsley's entire stock. Incidentally, we have to thank Dave Tooth, of Patshull, for the catchy name.

1   Orange Puppy Lure

COMMENT

Use the Orange Puppy in the conditions described for other orange lures, but when fishing coloured water early or late in the season, tie on a dropper two metres away from the point. I have taken some great catches when I have added a size 10 Viva to the dropper. Takes are about 50/50 on each, but the combination of the two makes a perfect team.

DRESSING

Hook: Size 8 long-shank leaded to a carrot shape.
Tying silk: Black.
Tail: Orange marabou.
Body: Fluorescent light orange chenille.
Head: Fluorescent red chenille.
Eyes: Bead links from a bath chain coated with white Cellire varnish with red dots added when the varnish is dry.

2   Blue Puppy Lure

COMMENT

This isn't a lure I favour, yet my son, Stephen, often proves me wrong where the colour blue is concerned. I was once fishing with Steve and not doing very well when he came up to me looking pleased with himself and asked how I was doing. Mind you, he knew the answer! To cut a long story short, he had caught a limit-bag on a blue pattern. I reluctantly tied one on and caught two trout – and I thought I knew all the answers!

DRESSING

Hook: Size 8 long-shank leaded to a carrot shape.
Tying silk: Black.
Tail: Blue marabou.
Body: Fluorescent blue chenille.
Head: Fluorescent pink chenille.
Eyes: Bead links from a bath chain coated with white Cellire varnish with red dots added when the varnish is dry.

1 Orange　**2** Blue　**3** Black　**4** Red
5 Pink　**6** White　**7** Yellow　**8** Green

3 Black Puppy Lure

COMMENT

You don't need me to tell you how effective black is, but add a pinch of fluorescent green and you have the deadly Viva combination. This version of the Puppy has been successful both at Patshull Park and many other Midlands fisheries.

DRESSING

Hook: Size 8 long-shank leaded to a carrot shape.
Tying silk: Black.
Tail: Black marabou.
Body: Black chenille.
Head: Fluorescent green chenille.
Eyes: Bead links from a bath chain coated with white Cellire varnish with red dots added when the varnish is dry.

4 Red Puppy Lure

COMMENT

This is a rare colour scheme and an unknown quantity to me. After I had suggested it would never catch trout, John Golding caught a heavyweight limit-bag on it from Leominstead. The best of it was that the tail had fallen off after the first two fish, but John had persevered and caught the rest on just the body! Either he is an exceptional fly-fisher or the trout couldn't see very well in the early-season peat-stained water. No offence, John!

DRESSING

Hook: Size 8 long-shank leaded to a carrot shape.
Tying silk: Black.
Tail: Red marabou.
Body: Fluorescent red chenille.
Head: Fluorescent green chenille.
Eyes: Bead links from a bath chain coated with white Cellire varnish with red dots added when the varnish is dry.

5 Pink Puppy Lure

COMMENT

Pink has earned a good reputation with the capture of large numbers of rainbow trout to good size in the early 1980s. Previously you might have been thought soft in the head to be seen fishing with such a 'nasty'. In fact, the lures have been christened 'Pink Nasties', but they do catch a lot of trout, especially when not over-used.

DRESSING

Hook: Size 8 long-shank leaded to a carrot shape.
Tying silk: Black.
Tail: Fluorescent pink marabou.
Body: Fluorescent light pink chenille.
Head: Fluorescent dark pink chenille.
Eyes: Bead links from a bath chain coated with white Cellire varnish with red dots added when the varnish is dry.

6 White Puppy Lure

COMMENT

When Dave Tooth introduced the Puppy series, I heard them described by many names including Muppets. These slightly gimmicky-looking patterns were not taken too seriously at first, but then curiosity got the better of a number of fly-fishers and they tried them. Then everyone started to take notice. The idea is yet another adaptation of the leaded lure to be fished singly on a No 8 line and quite powerful fly-rod in order to cast the lure a reasonable distance. This white pattern works well on most waters and is possibly taken for a small fish.

DRESSING

Hook: Size 8 long-shank leaded to a carrot shape.
Tying silk: Black.
Tail: White marabou.
Body: Fluorescent white chenille.
Head: Fluorescent red chenille.
Eyes: Bead links from a bath chain coated with white Cellire varnish with red dots added when the varnish is dry.

7 Yellow Puppy Lure

COMMENT

This lure looks incredible in the water and is a 'must' when you are in despair at what to try in coloured water. Although it might well scare trout in clear water, it is one to keep for use in dirty conditions.

DRESSING

Hook: Size 8 long-shank leaded to a carrot shape.
Tying silk: Black.
Tail: Bright yellow marabou.
Body: Fluorescent yellow chenille.
Head: Fluorescent orange chenille.
Eyes: Bead links from a bath chain coated with white Cellire varnish with red dots added when the varnish is dry.

8 Green Puppy Lure

COMMENT

I once caught a 3½lb Draycote brown trout which had two large frogs in its stomach. I imagine this lure would be good on a water where you know trout feed similarly at certain times of the year. I have little practical experience of this one, except that I did catch a trout on it from the Lechlade Fishery.

DRESSING

Hook: Size 8 long-shank leaded to a carrot-shape.
Tying silk: Black.
Tail: Green marabou.
Body: Fluorescent green chenille.
Head: Fluorescent red chenille.
Eyes: Bead links from a bath chain coated with white Cellire varnish with red dots added when the varnish is dry.

Tandem Lures

These are specialist lures intended to be fished deep-down on ledges and drop-offs around a reservoir on lead-impregnated or lead-core lines. Using them is in many cases an 'all or nothing' tactic, but it can be most rewarding when at the end of the day you weigh in a real heavyweight catch. I have known an exception to the rule, however. I remember once catching a very hungry trout of no more that eight inches on a six-inch tandem. That's fishing!

1   Black Muddler Tandem Special

COMMENT

This lure is especially for fishing along the bottom. A lead-core line is a must and drifting bow-first on the rudder gives the best presentation. On a reservoir, in a strong wind and a big wave, you can work up a good speed drifting in this manner. At such times you can troll the lure on 30 to 40 yards of line.

DRESSING

Hooks: Size 8 or 6 long-shank tandem mount.
Tying silk: Black.
Body: Black wool or chenille on both hooks.
Wings: Black marabou on both hooks.
Head: One or two of natural deerhair.

2   White and Silver Tandem Special

COMMENT

This is the original version of a White Tandem Lure, and it has caught trout for many anglers in its time. However, I have to say that some of the more recent developments along similar lines are far better fish-catchers.

DRESSING

Hooks: Size 8 or 6 medium-shank tandem mount.
Tying silk: Black.
Bodies: Silver tinsel.
Hackle: White cock on front hook only.
Wings: Four long white cock hackles.
Heads: Black varnish.

1 Black Muddler   **2** White and Silver   **3** White Muddler   **4** Pearl and White
5 Appetiser   **6** Leprechaun   **7** Whisky   **8** Goldie

3 White Muddler Tandem Special

COMMENT

This is another good fry-imitating lure. Mick Nicholls, from Coventry, and I had some excellent catches on it from Grafham in the early 1970s. On a couple of occasions we shared 40lb-plus double-limits while fishing from anchor at the aeration tower. We anchored 30 metres from the tower and cast with lead-core lines so that our lures hit the stonework. The water here is 25 feet deep, and the lines sank quickly, followed slowly by the buoyant tandem White Muddler. We had many takes on the drop, with a best rainbow of 5lb.

DRESSING

Hooks: Size 8 or 6 long-shank tandem mount.
Tying silk: Black.
Bodies: White fluorescent Baby Doll wool on both hooks.
Wings: White marabou on both hooks.
Heads: One or two. White deerhair.

4 Pearl and White Tandem Special

COMMENT

With the arrival of pearl body materials, some excellent new patterns were developed in the 1984-85 seasons. Many have not yet reached their true potential, but I can vouch for this one working at Pitsford, Grafham and Rutland. I am looking forward to trying it in ideal circumstances.

DRESSING

Hooks: Size 8 or 6 long-shank tandem mount.
Tying silk: Black.
Tail: Fluorescent green cock hackle-fibres.
Bodies: Pearl Bobbydazzlelure.
Wing: Long white bucktail topped with green Flashabou on front hook. No wing on rear hook.
Heads: Black varnish.

5 Appetiser Tandem Special

COMMENT

This is another of my patterns, and a natural follow-on from the successful single-hook version. I believe it to be one of the best coarse-fish fry imitations yet devised. It is the pattern to use once trout begin to feed on the larger fry. Fish it singly on a long 7lb breaking-strain leader.

DRESSING

Hooks: Size 8 or 6 long-shank tandem mount.
Tying silk: Black.
Tails: Orange, green and silver mallard hackle-fibres on both hooks.
Bodies: White chenille ribbed with silver oval tinsel on both hooks.
Hackles: Orange, green and silver mallard hackle-fibres on both hooks.
Underwings: White marabou.
Overwings: Natural long squirrel-tail hair.
Heads: Black varnish.

6 Leprechaun Tandem Special

COMMENT

It was on this lure that I hooked, and lost, the largest fish I have ever had on while boat-fishing at Rutland Water. I was about 100 metres out from the point of Hambleton Peninsula, fishing deep-down on a rudder drift, when I hooked the powerful unseen fish. I played it for more than ten minutes before it slipped the hook and escaped, still unseen.

DRESSING

Hooks: Size 8 or 6 long-shank tandem mount.
Tying silk: Black.
Tail: Green hackle-fibres.
Bodies: Green chenille ribbed with silver tinsel.
Wings: Green bucktail.
Hackle: Green cock.
Heads: Black varnish.

7 Whisky Tandem Special

COMMENT

I once saw Alan Pearson catch four fine rainbows on this lure from Walton Hall lake in a morning session in 'impossible' conditions. It was early season and we had had so much rain that the water was like milky coffee. I honestly thought we would blank, yet when I tried a similar lure on a sinking line I, too, caught my limit.

DRESSING

Hooks: Size 8 or 6 long-shank tandem mount.
Tying silk: Orange.
Tails: Red floss on both hooks.
Bodies: Red floss ribbed with gold tinsel on both hooks.
Hackle: Hot-orange cock on both hooks.
Wings: Orange bucktail on both hooks.
Heads: Clear varnish.

8 Goldie Tandem Special

COMMENT

This pattern, which I devised for Rutland, works extremely well for brown trout when used either as a tandem or as a single. However, the tandem version certainly catches the larger fish, and it has accounted for many of between 4lb and 6lb. Use it on a fast-sinking or lead-core line for the best results.

DRESSING

Hooks: Size 8 or 6 long-shank tandem mount.
Tying silk: Black.
Tails: Yellow hackle-fibres on both hooks.
Bodies: Gold tinsel ribbed with gold wire on both hooks.
Underwings: Yellow goat-hair or bucktail on both hooks.
Overwings: Black goat-hair or bucktail on both hooks.
Heads: Black varnish.

Special Lures

The Waggy lures probably only just qualify as legal, but they have become very popular on the reservoirs. The Cat's Whisker proved so deadly for me during the first two months of last year that one day I had to take it off. The first time it was tried by its inventor David Train, of Swindon, it caught fish to 10¼lb from Willow Pool at Linch Hill. On a second visit, David broke the fishery record for a four-fish limit-bag: 14¼lb, 14lb, 12½lb and 5lb. He caught three of the four fish by spotting them, casting close to them, and seeing the takes – exciting fishing!

1 Palmer-eyed Viva

COMMENT

This is another lure introduced to me by former *Trout and Salmon* Editor, John Wilshaw. John was catching and releasing rainbows at Gerald Denton's super small fishery at Cleatham, near Scunthorpe. I had been catching at about half John's rate, but I soon began to catch up after I coaxed him into giving me one of these lures. This pattern has since been impressive whenever I have tried it.

DRESSING

Hook: Size 6 long-shank.
Tying silk: Black.
Tail: Black marabou.
Body: Fluorescent green chenille at rear; then black chenille ribbed with silver tinsel.
Body hackle: Black long-fibred cock, palmered.
Head: Large chain bead eyes.

2 Yellow Waggy

COMMENT

Although the original Waggy was a white, fish-imitating lure, a set of four have gradually become popular. This yellow version is a good one to try in coloured or peaty water.

DRESSING

Hook: Size 6 long-shank.
Tying silk: Black.
Tail: Yellow rubber 'waggy' tail.
Body: Fluorescent yellow chenille ribbed with gold tinsel.
Hackle: Yellow cock.
Wing: Yellow marabou.
Head: Black varnish with eyes painted on.

1 Palmer-eyed Viva   **2** Yellow Waggy   **3** Bullet Minnow   **4** White Waggy
5 Cat's Whisker   **6** Orange Waggy   **7** Exocet   **8** Black Waggy

3 Bullet Minnow

COMMENT

This is the most realistic fry imitation to come from America, and is a first-class lure to use at the back-end of the season. Although a little difficult to tie, it is well worth the effort. Fish it on either a floating or a sinking line. It is best fished from the banks of reservoirs in September and October, with shallow, weedy areas giving the best results.

DRESSING

Hook: Size 8, 6 or 4 extra-long-shank.
Tying silk: Red.
Body: Silver tinsel.
Overhead wing and tail: Natural brown bucktail.
Underhead wing and tail: White bucktail. Tie off hair with red silk a third of the way down body. Finish with high clear varnish and transfer or painted-on eyes.

4 White Waggy

COMMENT

Fred Wagstaffe introduced this controversial lure to Rutland and obtained permission to use it. It imitates a swimming fish better than any other lure. Some anglers questioned its legality at the time, but most Rutland regulars now have a few 'Waggies'. It would seem that the pattern is allowed at most stillwaters.

DRESSING

Hook: Size 6 long-shank.
Tying silk: Black.
Tail: White rubber 'waggy' tail.
Body: White chenille ribbed with silver tinsel.
Hackle: White cock.
Wing: White marabou.
Head: Black varnish with eyes painted on.

5 Cat's Whisker

COMMENT

The Cat's Whisker, invented by David Train was one of the big successes of 1985. After getting many short takes while fishing at Ringstead Grange, David decided to modify the standard Tadpole-type dressing. As well as the white marabou tail, he added a white marabou wing in the hope that the trout would hit the lure closer to the head and consequently be hooked. To stop the wing looping round the hook-shank, David added four white cat's whiskers shed by his pet cat, hence the name. Use it singly or with a small dropper on a floating or sinking line.

DRESSING

Hook: Size 6 long-shank.
Tying silk: Black.
Tail: White marabou.
Body: Fluorescent yellow chenille ribbed with silver oval tinsel.
Wing: White marabou.
Head: Large chain bead eyes.

6 Orange Waggy

COMMENT

Like most orange-based lures, this one works best during the hot summer months. Make long casts downwind with a floating shooting-head and then strip the lure back very fast across the surface. The takes from rainbows will nearly pull the rod out of your hand.

DRESSING

Hook: Size 6 long-shank.
Tying silk: Black.
Tail: Orange rubber 'waggy' tail.
Body: Orange chenille ribbed with gold tinsel.
Hackle: Orange cock.
Wing: Orange marabou.
Head: Black varnish with eyes painted on.

7 Exocet

COMMENT

Professional fly-tyer Robin Hayden devised this lure and sent me a couple to try. Like all outrageously gaudy lures, it seems to catch rainbows very well. Robin tells me the lure was successful throughout the 1985 season on most of the Gloucestershire gravel-pit fisheries.

DRESSING

Hook: Size 6 long-shank.
Tying silk: Black.
Tail: Yellow marabou.
Body: Fluorescent lime-green chenille ribbed with gold wire.
Body hackle: Black long-fibred cock, palmered.
Head: Fluorescent pink chenille.

8 Black Waggy

COMMENT

This black leech-imitating pattern was a natural follow-on to the white version. Fish it deep on a lead-impregnated fly-line so that the lure works along the bottom for a good distance. It is therefore a good idea to use a shooting-head, so that you can cast much greater distances.

DRESSING

Hook: Size 6 long-shank.
Tying silk: Black.
Tail: Black rubber 'waggy' tail.
Body: Fluorescent green blob near tail; then black chenille ribbed with silver tinsel.
Hackle: Black cock.
Wing: Black marabou.
Head: Black varnish with eyes painted on.

Buoyant Lures

Buoyant lures are the new craze for fishing the big reservoirs at the back-end of the season in September and October. This new dry-fly lure-fishing technique certainly sorts out the big, old fish, which love to feed on fry at this time.

1 Fireball

COMMENT

The name speaks for itself, and this new lure is unsinkable. To fish it with any success you need to have a fair wave on a rainbow-stocked reservoir. Cast downwind from a broadside-drifting boat and strip the lure back through the waves as you would a Muddler. It is one to try in the summer.

DRESSING

Hook: Size 6 long-shank.
Tying silk: Black.
Tail: Orange and yellow marabou.
Underbody: Buoyant Ethafoam strip.
Overbody: Fluorescent white chenille.
Head: Black varnish.

2 Muddler-head Tube

COMMENT

The object of this Muddler-head Tube-fly is to enable you to change any normal lure into a Muddler. All you do is slide the Muddler tube up the trace and tie on your favourite lure. For example, a Black Chenille lure would become a Black Muddler, a Jack Frost a White Muddler, a Church Fry an Orange Muddler, and so on.

DRESSING

Hook: None.
Tying silk: Black.
Body: Half-inch plastic tube with spun natural deerhair throughout its length, clipped to selected shape.

1 Fireball   **2** Muddler-head Tube   **3** Dead-fish Tube Lure   **4** Deerhair Vole
5 Wiggly   **6** Ethafoam Dead Roach   **7** Dying Fry   **8** Injured/Ailing Fry

3 Dead-fish Tube Lure

COMMENT

Although tube-flies have been used regularly by lead-core line anglers, this is the first I have seen for surface fishing. Like the normal lure, it should be fished on the surface and simply allowed to drift with the breeze. When a trout takes, it does so just as it would go for a small dry fly, but the treble hook ensures good hooking qualities on such a large lure. Trout often feed on small roach or perch of this size at the back-end.

DRESSING

Hook: Independent treble, size 10 or 8.
Tying silk: Black or white.
Body: Pearl or silver Mylar on plastic tube of preferred length (three inches is suggested).
Hackle: Crimson cock fibres.
Tail and Back: White Ethafoam, cut to shape.
Tube end: Add a strip of red latex rubber tube to take the shank of the treble.

4 Deerhair Vole

COMMENT

This fancy pattern shows just what can be done with deerhair. It is not a pattern I would use regularly, but I have caught fish on it. In the early days of Grafham, soon after the Muddler was introduced by Tom Saville, my friends and I tied up some of these large lures. The big 'wild' rainbows of that never-to-be-forgotten period would take them when a good wind was on – and from the bank, too.

DRESSING

Hook: Size 4 extra-long-shank.
Tying silk: White.
Tail: Thick black nylon wool.
Body: Natural deerhair clipped to shape.
Eyes: Red beads.
Head: Tapered and finished with clear varnish.

5 Wiggly

COMMENT

This is basically a fry imitation which can be fished as a wake fly or as a static drifter. Because it is like a Muddler, it will work when fished in a similar manner. I was given the pattern by a Rutland angler who told me of his good catches on it. The tail takes on a 'wiggly' action when the lure is pulled over the surface – hence the name.

DRESSING

Hook: Size 6 or 4 long-shank.
Tying silk: White.
Tail: White marabou.
Body: White deerhair clipped to shape.
Thorax: Red deerhair clipped to shape.
Head: Clear varnish.

6 Ethafoam Dead Roach

COMMENT

This is a super floating-fry pattern developed for Rutland. It is best fished on a size 9 or 10 floating shooting-head, so that it can be cast good distances and allowed to drift with the wind towards the nearest weed-bed. It is better if the pearl Myler is oversize, so that it can be compressed to give a realistic, pot-bellied effect before it is secured with the tying silk.

DRESSING

Hook: Size 6 or 4 long-shank.
Tying silk: White.
Body: Pearl Mylar.
Tail and back: White Ethafoam cut to shape.
Head: Clear varnish.

7 Dying Fry

COMMENT

Fish this one singly on the surface. Cast it close to a weed-bed and retrieve it very slowly with a series of short twitches to impart action and the impression of life to the marabou in the tail. This method would have been laughed at a few years ago, yet today it is recognised as the best approach for catching those big 'wild' reservoir trout at the back-end.

DRESSING

Hook: Size 4 nickel extra-long-shank.
Tying silk: Black.
Tail: Red marabou.
Underbody: Strip of Ethafoam for buoyancy.
Overbody: Pearl Bobbydazzlelure.
Back: Bronze peacock herl.
Gills: Pair of red cock hackle-tips.
Head: Black varnish. Eyes optional.

8 Injured/Ailing Fry

COMMENT

A number of the yearling perch and roach begin to die off at the back-end of the season, and the big trout seem to sort out these injured or ailing fry as food as they hunt the shallow, weedy areas of a reservoir. Fish this lure on the surface with an irregular stop-start retrieve. This can be speeded up if trout show interest, but will not take. The action in the tail and wings gives the impression of life.

DRESSING

Hook: Size 4 nickel extra-long-shank.
Tying silk: Black.
Tail: Bronze peacock points.
Underbody: Strip of Ethafoam for buoyancy.
Overbody: Pearl Bobbydazzlelure.
Hackle: Orange cock fibres.
Underwing: White marabou.
Overwing: Long grey squirrel-tail hair.
Eyes: Imitation jungle cock.
Head: Black varnish.

Highly-visible Lures

This set of fancy lures incorporating fluorescent and phosphorescent or luminous materials is a major breakthrough. Trials in 1984 and 1985 showed that they have great potential. When you think about it, it seems to make sense to use such materials. For much of the time our lures are fished deep-down in the murky depths, where visibility is low. In theory, a bright glowing lure should attract more fish, and indeed, in practice this has proved to be so. You must try them.

1   Julian's Rutland Lure

COMMENT

This lure was introduced to Rutland by Leicester angler Julian Hubbard, who has taken some fine catches of big fish on it by using a lead-core line and rudder-drifting tactics. The lure is allowed to sink right to the bottom before it is stripped back very fast. In May 1985 my son, Steve, using this lure, was leading me six-nil at Rutland while we were boat-fishing. It wasn't until he hooked the bottom and lost it that I was able to catch up. I was impressed.

DRESSING

Hook: Independent treble, size 8 or 10.
Tying silk: Black.
Body: Silver Mylar on a plastic tube (one or two inches), with a strip of red latex rubber tube at tail.
Wing: Gold and silver Mylar mixed after unthreading.
Hackle: Hot-orange.
Eyes: Painted on.

2   Light-bulb Lure

COMMENT

If you think some other lures are bright, you should see this one! It's like a neon sign! When I was experimenting with this phosphorescent material, I figured it would work well when included in the dressing of a lure fished at depths of thirty feet or more. The lure is luminous in the dark and that's what it is like in those murky reservoir depths. It worked well in early tests, but I have yet to complete my findings.

DRESSING

Hook: Size 8 or 6 long-shank.
Tying silk: Black.
Tail: Fluorescent yellow marabou, generous.
Body: Fluorescent yellow chenille.
Wing: Phosphorescent ivory Flashabou.
Head: White deerhair.

1 Julian's Rutland Lure   **2** Light-bulb Lure   **3** Luminous Fry   **4** Pearl Flashabou Fry
5 Fluorescent Orange Lure   **6** Blue Lou   **7** Davy Wotton's Fancy Lure   **8** Geronimo

3 Luminous Fry

COMMENT

This is another lure which is luminous in the dark or in deep water. The new phosphorescent Flashabou has many uses, including the ribbing on nymphs and wet-flies. This lure should be a good early-season pattern in its small sizes when the water is still murky – a lure of the future.

DRESSING

Hook: Size 10, 8 or 6 long-shank.
Tying silk: Black.
Tail: White marabou.
Body: Pearl Bobbydazzlelure.
Underwing: Fluorescent white marabou.
Overwing: Phosphorescent green Flashabou.
Hackle: Orange cock.
Head: Black varnish.

4 Pearl Flashabou Fry

COMMENT

This is one of the new brand of fry-imitating lures. In 1985 everyone went overboard on the new pearl materials, for it was found that some fine patterns could be devised once they were mixed with white marabou. This one, with pearl in both tail and body, seems to have great potential as a catcher of big fish.

DRESSING

Hook: Size 8 or 6 long-shank.
Tying silk: Black.
Tail: White marabou.
Body: Pearl Bobbydazzlelure.
Underwing: White marabou.
Overwing: Pearl Flashabou.
Hackle: Kingfisher-blue cock fibres.
Head: Black varnish.

5 Fluorescent Orange Lure

COMMENT

Skunk-tail hair is rarely used, yet it makes a good wing material. This lure is at its best fished on a slow-sinking or sink-tip line from June to September. Try fishing two on the cast and stripping back as fast as you can on the downwind side of the reservoir.

DRESSING

Hook: Size 10, 8 or 6 long-shank.
Tying silk: Black.
Tail: Tip from French partridge hackle dyed yellow.
Body: Fluorescent orange chenille.
Underwing: Fluorescent orange marabou.
Overwing: Dyed orange skunk-tail hair.
Hackle: Orange cock.
Head: Black varnish.

6 Blue Lou

COMMENT

My son is once again responsible for this blue lure, which, as we who fish with him have grudgingly to admit, works very well. My downfall was asking him for one to try one day when he was doing pretty well. He's never let me forget it. He admits his ambition is to persuade International fly-fisher Brian Leadbetter to use one.

DRESSING

Hook: Size 10 or 8, single or double, leaded.
Tying silk: Black.
Tail: Kingfisher-blue marabou.
Body: Copper Bobbydazzlelure.
Wing: Kingfisher-blue marabou.
Head: Pearl Bobbydazzlelure.
Head finish: Black varnish.

7 Davy Wotton's Fancy Lure

COMMENT

Davy gave me this original fancy lure some time back and it sat in my fly-box for about four seasons. I did christen it one day at Rutland and caught a decent rainbow on a sinking line. I washed the lure well, allowed it to dry, and then put it back in the box, where it has been ever since.

DRESSING

Hook: Size 4, extra-long-shank.
Tying silk: Black.
Tail: Two yellow and two black cock hackles with a pinch of yellow bucktail.
Body: Black chenille.
Wings: Pair of Plymouth Rock cock hackles, black cock hackles in the centre.
Hackle: Yellow marabou.
Cheeks: Teal breast feather.
Head: Green and black chenille.
Eyes: Bath-chain beads.
Head: Black varnish.

8 Geronimo

COMMENT

It is rare to see nymph specialist Brian Harris using a lure, so it is surprising to know that he invented this one. It was his alternative to a Muddler Minnow, which he did not rate highly. Brian's bright lure works well in the main summer months, when it should be fished fast on a floating line.

DRESSING

Hook: Size 10, 8 or 6 long-shank.
Tying silk: Black.
Tail: Mixed brown and yellow cock hackle-fibres.
Body: Gold Bobbydazzlelure.
Wing: Four cree cock hackles.
Rear hackle: Two turns of long-fibred orange cock.
Front hackle: Two turns of yellow cock.
Head: Black varnish.

Hairwing Lures

These patterns, new in 1985, all have hairwings instead of hackles or marabou. Early tests showed they were as good as any from the past, and perhaps better. Hairwings were all the rage in the 1960s, but fashions change and a new trend was set when I introduced marabou with my Appetiser lure. However, I still tend to prefer hairwing patterns, and have the utmost faith in their fish-catching abilities. This is a selection of quite rare patterns. I bet you won't know many of these!

1 Assassin

COMMENT

This new trout lure has a salmon background. I am not too sure of this one yet, other than I caught four fish on it after about twenty lure changes. Whether that was luck or not, only time will tell. Let's say it has started well.

DRESSING

Hook: Size 8 or 6 long-shank.
Tying silk: Black.
Tail: Yellow hackle-tips.
Body: Silver Bobbydazzlelure.
Body hackle: Yellow cock.
Hackle: Silver mallard breast.
Wing: Light brown deerhair.
Head: Black varnish.

2 GBH Lure

COMMENT

A lure incorporating the colours of a nasty bruise could hardly have any other name. It is a general lure pattern to be fished on a sinking line. Use a size 10 in early season, progressing to the larger sizes as the water warms up.

DRESSING

Hook: Size 10, 8 or 6 long-shank.
Tying silk: Black.
Tail: Yellow hackle-fibres.
Body: Rear — yellow midge floss. Front — black suede chenille ribbed with gold tinsel.
Wing: Black bucktail hair.
Hackle: Kingfisher-blue cock.
Head: Black varnish.

1 Assassin   **2** GBH Lure   **3** Yellow Meannie   **4** Integration Lure
5 Copper Sunset   **6** Red-bead Lure   **7** Apricot Lil   **8** Black Maria

3 Yellow Meannie

COMMENT

This one is from Brian Furzer. He had the idea for it after reading a book by the American writer and fly-fisherman, Joe Brookes. It is a variant of his Honey Blonde, and Brian has caught many fine browns up to 6lb-plus from Grafham on it. The method is to fish it deep and slow on a lead-impregnated shooting-head line.

DRESSING

Hook: Size 8, 6, 4 or 2 long-shank.
Tying silk: Black.
Tail: Yellow bucktail.
Body: Gold Bobbydazzlelure.
Wing: Yellow bucktail.
Head: Black varnish.

4 Integration Lure

COMMENT

This pattern is from America, but the all-important colours of black, white and orange work equally well with trout in British waters. The lure can be fished either as a fry-imitator or as an attractor on a floating or a sinking line.

DRESSING

Hook: Size 6, 8 or 10 long-shank bronze.
Tying silk: Black.
Tail: Orange goat-hair or bucktail.
Body: Silver tinsel ribbed with silver oval tinsel.
Hackle: White hackle-fibres. Throat only.
Wing: White goat-hair or bucktail at the bottom, then black in the centre, followed by white again for the wing top. This gives a badger-hackle effect.

5 Copper Sunset

COMMENT

This lure is so pleasing to a fly-dresser's eyes that it just has to be good at catching trout! I experimented with it during the 1985 season and was more than pleased with the results. It worked well on a sinking line in the colder months, but in July and August it fished well three to four feet down on a slow-sinker when a lot of daphnia were about.

DRESSING

Hook: Size 12, 10, 8 or 6 long-shank.
Tying silk: Black.
Body: Copper Bobbydazzlelure.
Underwing: Black bucktail.
Overwing: Orange bucktail.
Head: Black varnish.

6   Red-bead Lure

COMMENT

This is one of Syd Brock's Farmoor I and II patterns. Syd has now moved away from his beloved reservoirs, but in his day he was one of the best reservoir men around. He had several large fish to his credit including a 10lb brown trout from Farmoor I. This lure was designed for midsummer fishing for rainbows.

DRESSING

Hook: Size 12, 10 or 8 long-shank.
Tying silk: Black.
Body: Red floss covered in stretched clear polythene strip.
Hackle: Orange cock.
Wing: Red bucktail or goat-hair topped with silver mallard.
Head: Bright red bead with eyes painted on.

7   Apricot Lil

COMMENT

Leicester fly-fisher Tony Wadsworth gave me this lure back in the mid-1970s. He was feeling pretty good at the time, for he had just won the Gladding Masters at Draycote reservoir. The lure is in the same family as the deadly Whisky Fly, and instructions for fishing it are the same.

DRESSING

Hook: Size 10, 8 or 6 long-shank.
Tying silk: Orange.
Tail: Golden-pheasant tippets.
Body: Orange ostrich herl ribbed with gold tinsel.
Hackle: Orange cock.
Underwing: Mixed orange marabou and goat-hair.
Overwing: Dyed orange squirrel-tail hair.
Head: Clear varnish.

8   Black Maria

COMMENT

The Black Maria has a colour scheme similar to that of the Goldie, the top Rutland lure. It was little wonder, then, to find that this lure worked well at the big reservoirs. Results were good when it was fished deep on a lead-core line from a rudder-drifting boat.

DRESSING

Hook: Size 10, 8 or 6 long-shank.
Tying silk: Black.
Tail: Yellow cock hackle-fibres.
Tag: Silver tinsel.
Body: Rear – fluorescent yellow chenille. Front – black suede chenille, ribbed with silver tinsel.
Hackle: Natural black cock.
Wing: Black marabou.
Head: Black varnish.

Ugly Ducklings

This may seem a strange name for a series of flies, but they proved a tremendous success for me in 1985, and I heard of some good catches on them early in the 1986 season. Naturally, the different colours are for different fishing situations and conditions. They should be fished fast through the top during summer, or slow and deep early in the season. I'm still quietly smug about this little collection.

1 Yellow Ugly Duckling

COMMENT

The yellow version of this new series of flies is one to try on a sinking line. Early-season stock rainbows are keen to grab it, making it worth trying in April and May. A fast-sinking line can be used even if the water is quite shallow, for there is little weed-growth in these early months.

DRESSING

Hook: Size 12 or 10.
Tying silk: Black.
Tail: Yellow hackle-fibres.
Body: Gold Bobbydazzlelure.
Head: Fluorescent yellow chenille.
Wing: Yellow marabou or four hackle-tips.
Head finish: Black varnish.

2 Red Ugly Duckling

COMMENT

Red, once a rarely-used colour, has slowly been creeping into a number of new fly patterns during the 1980s. The time to try this pattern is when one or two flies have been popular at a water for a couple of weeks or more. I long ago proved that it pays to keep one step ahead of the majority with fly-changes and colours.

DRESSING

Hook: Size 12 or 10.
Tying silk: Black.
Tail: Red cock hackle-fibres.
Body: Pearl Bobbydazzlelure.
Head: Fluorescent red chenille.
Wing: Red marabou or four red cock hackle-tips.
Head finish: Black varnish.

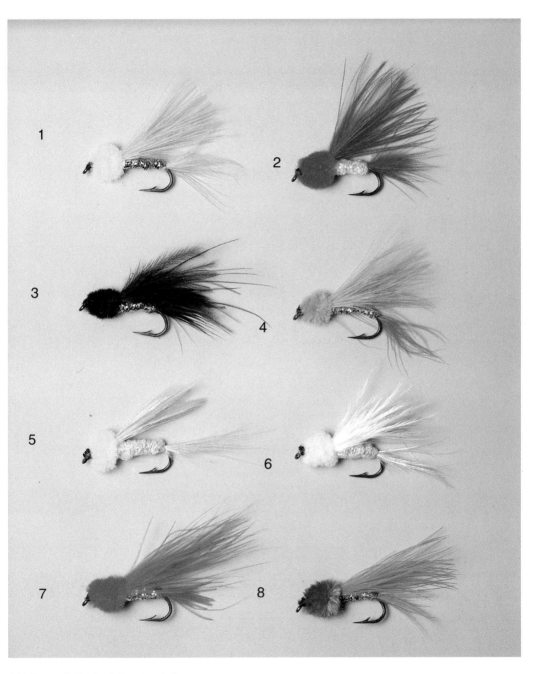

1 Yellow **2** Red **3** Black **4** Orange
5 Lime-green **6** White **7** Pink **8** Blue

3 Black Ugly Duckling

COMMENT

The excellent colour combination of black and gold is at its best here. The bulky chenille head gives off a Muddler-type wake when the lure is retrieved fast, and this helps to attract trout. This pattern may be fished with confidence on a sinking line from March to the end of May.

DRESSING

Hook: Size 12 or 10.
Tying silk: Black.
Tail: Black cock hackle-fibres.
Body: Gold Bobbydazzlelure.
Head: Black suede chenille.
Wing: Black marabou or four black cock hackle-tips.
Head finish: Black varnish.

4 Orange Ugly Duckling

COMMENT

My favourite summer pattern of the Ugly Duckling series is the Orange dressing. It has caught many fish for me, nearly all of them rainbows. My three most effective summer surface flies which include the deadly orange colour are Peach Doll, Old Nick and this Orange Ugly Duckling, which works well from June to September. Use it as a point-fly on a team of wets and fish it as you would a Muddler.

DRESSING

Hook: Size 12 or 10.
Tying silk: Black.
Tail: Hot-orange cock hackle-fibres.
Body: Gold Bobbydazzlelure.
Head: Fluorescent orange chenille.
Wing: Orange marabou or four hackle-fibres.
Head finish: Black varnish.

5 Lime-green Ugly Duckling

COMMENT

An old Norfolk fly-fisherman once wrote to me saying that the fluorescent version of a size 10 Leprechaun had been giving him the best catches of his life. He wasn't talking only about easy stock rainbows. He named several waters, including small fisheries, reservoirs, and Scottish lochs and rivers on which he had been successful. This Duckling has that important fluorescent lime-green teamed up with the new top body colour, pearl. Early tests with it have been impressive.

DRESSING

Hook: Size 12 or 10.
Tying silk: Black.
Tail: Fluorescent lime-green hackle-fibres.
Body: Pearl Bobbydazzlelure.
Head: Fluorescent lime-green chenille.
Wing: Fluorescent lime-green marabou or four hackle-tips.
Head finish: Black varnish.

6 White Ugly Duckling

COMMENT

The Ugly Duckling series was the first to incorporate the new Bobbydazzlelure body material. For the first time we have, as well as the main colours (silver, gold and copper) a pearl body material that can be wound on instead of being slid on to the hook-shank in tubular form. The new material is more rugged and does not tear so easily on the trout's teeth as does the Mylar tube. This white version is a first-class mini fry-imitator.

DRESSING

Hook: Size 12 or 10.
Tying silk: Black.
Tail: Fluorescent white hackle-fibres.
Body: Pearl Bobbydazzlelure.
Head: Fluorescent white chenille.
Wing: White marabou or four cock hackle-tips.
Head finish: Black varnish.

7 Pink Ugly Duckling

COMMENT

Like other pink flies, this one may look 'shocking' to the traditionalist, but it has a purpose – to 'shock' rainbow trout into taking. The colour seems to arouse the aggressive instinct in rainbows, especially from May to September when water temperatures are high. The lure may be fished on a floating or a sinking line.

DRESSING

Hook: Size 12 or 10.
Tying silk: Black.
Tail: Fluorescent pink cock hackle-fibres.
Body: Silver Bobbydazzlelure.
Head: Fluorescent pink chenille.
Wing: Pink marabou or four fluorescent pink cock hackle-tips.
Head finish: Black varnish.

8 Blue Ugly Duckling

COMMENT

On opening day at Ringstead Grange fishery in 1985, everyone was catching quite well, but by midday word had passed round the 35-acre lake that one angler had caught a brace of 7lb rainbows on a blue lure. As I was on one side of the lake and my son Steve (keen on blue lures) was on the other, I put two and two together and thought, 'Well done Steve!' However, when I met up with him for lunch, it wasn't Steve but another angler who, like him, had a passion for bright blue flies.

DRESSING

Hook: Size 12 or 10.
Tying silk: Black.
Tail: Blue cock hackle-fibres.
Body: Gold Bobbydazzlelure.
Head: Fluorescent blue chenille.
Wing: Fluorescent blue marabou or four hackle-tips.
Head finish: Black varnish.

Important Originals

We have a really good mixture in this selection. Some of the patterns may be considered outrageous, yet they are all well-known trout-catchers. The Flash Bang Wallop caught the heaviest English fly-caught brown trout, 14½lb, for David Wood from Queen Mother Reservoir in 1985 when he was trying to find the rainbow shoals before a match. Having drawn blank on the Triangle Bank with a Caddis Nymph, he trolled over to the Far Bank, where, in his own words: 'the lead-core trolling line must have sunk to 30 feet before I started reeling in fast. I had about 100 yards of backing out when I noticed how my rod-tip was bouncing around. Suddenly, the rod bent and the reel handle was whipped out of my fingers. A few short runs and 10 minutes later I managed to guide the fish over my net. As I saw its size, it saw me, turned and leapt. This run was about 70 yards. The next five minutes was like a lifetime. Finally, under went the net just as the fish turned on its side – a brownie! My heart pounded as I used my priest. It was a shame, but nobody would have believed it without seeing it.'

1 Popping Bug (black version)

COMMENT

This is an American idea that is becoming popular in Britain. The bug works on a similar principle to that of another famous American pattern, the Muddler Minnow. It is cast as far as possible on a floating shooting-head and then retrieved in a series of fast, jerky pulls. Each time you pull, you will hear the 'pop' quite clearly as the lure skates across the surface. Super-fit summer and autumn rainbows are most attracted by this unique action. The Americans also use the Popping Bug for largemouth and smallmouth bass.

DRESSING

Hook: Size 8, 6 or 4 extra-long-shank bronze.
Body: A piece of balsa wood, its size according to the hook-size, half-bullet shape, with a concave 'scoop' out of the flat end. Make a hole so that a hook can be pushed through and use Superglue to hold it in position. Whip the shank with black tying silk close to the balsa, making a firm anchorage. Now tie in three or four cock hackle feathers, colour as required, and finally tie in two long-fibred hackles full circle.

2 Goat's Toe

COMMENT

I was introduced to this old and almost forgotten Irish fly by top Lincolnshire fly-fisher Terry Oliver. I found it a good top dropper fly, but it was the yellow-bodied, green-hackled pattern which was most effective until one day on Lough Carra. A few fish were rising and the reed-beds were thick with damselflies. Some were blown on to the water, and the trout were taking them. The blue-hackled Goat's Toe with a red body was the nearest imitation I had of the blue male fly. I put it on and took three 2lb browns in three casts. It is a fine sea-trout fly, too.

DRESSING

Hook: Size 12, 10 or 8.
Tying Silk: Black.
Tag: Gold or silver tinsel. It pays to experiment.
Tail: Red or yellow floss or wool.
Body: Red or yellow floss or wool closely ribbed with bronze peacock herl.
Hackle: Green or blue peacock breast feather.
Head: Black varnish.

1 Popping Bug   **2/2a** Goat's Toe   **3** Pearly   **4** Punk Rocker
5 Fred Wagstaffe's Coarse-fish Lure   **6** Concorde   **7** Balling Buzzer
8 Flash Bang Wallop

3 Pearly

COMMENT

Syd Brock has invented some very good flies and lures in his time, and this is one from a set which he calls his Pearlies. He liked the idea of the bulky Muddler head, but he substituted this with a pearl bead from one of his wife's old necklaces. This version is good when fished fast through the surface on a floating line. June to September are the best months for it.

DRESSING

Hook: Size 10 or 8 medium-shank.
Tying silk: Black.
Body: Orange floss ribbed with silver wire.
Hackle: Hot-orange. Throat only.
Underwing: Red goat-hair or similar.
Overwing: Silver mallard.
Head: Pearl bead painted red with painted eyes.

4 Punk Rocker

COMMENT

Mark Frost developed this pattern for Ringstead. He says: 'This fly can be fished on a floating or a sinking line and as a lure or as a nymph. I've had a lot of success with it on size 10 and 14 hooks and using it as a bob-fly. The heavy hackle gives plenty of movement to the fly when it is pulled through the water. When the damselfly is hatching, green, yellow and blue hackles seem to work well when other imitations fail. I called it the Punk Rocker because it reminded me of youths with spiked multi-coloured hairstyles.'

DRESSING

Hook: Size 14 to 8 long- or normal-shank.
Tying silk: Yellow.
Body: Yellow seal's fur, leaded if necessary.
Rib: Oval gold or wire, depending on size.
Hackle: Heavy palmered cock hackles. Yellow and various shades of green are best. Also use blue, yellow, green or any colour to suit your local water.

5 Fred Wagstaffe's Coarse-fish Lure

COMMENT

Fred Wagstaffe is the best deep-fisher I know. He has caught many fine brown trout from large, deep loughs, lochs and reservoirs, and holds the best-catch record at Rutland Water for a limit-bag of eight trout which weighed more than 50lb. He believes that large browns feed irregularly, but that when they do feed they like sizeable food items such as roach or perch of 4 – 6oz or even small stocked trout. This lure is fished from a boat on a lead-core line and worked along the bottom.

DRESSING

Hooks: Tandem. Front, size 2 long-shank, nickel-plated hook joined with a large loop of 30lb black nylon to a size 2 double salmon hook at rear.
Tying silk: Black.
Rear hook tail: Orange goat-hair.
Rear hook body: White chenille ribbed with silver tinsel.
Front hook body: White chenille ribbed with silver tinsel.
Wing: Long white bucktail or goat-hair.
Head: White deerhair, very prominent.

6 Concorde

COMMENT

This lure was a joint effort by Peter Gathercole and myself. Our idea was to have the flash part of the body as the main and easily-visible attractor, so it is not covered by hackle or wing-covers as it is in most lures. Our early tests at Rutland when using medium-sinking lines gave solid, positive takes from both rainbows and browns. This is a good pattern from mid-season onwards. Trout seem to have a go at it simply because it looks so different, and good catches have been made when traditional lures have failed.

DRESSING

Hook: Size 8 or 6 long-shank.
Tying silk: Black.
Tail and wing: Red bucktail and four selected Plymouth Rock cock hackles.
Hackle: Long-fibred crimson cock.
Body: Copper or gold Bobbydazzlelure.
Head: Black varnish.

7 Balling Buzzer

COMMENT

I was given this unusual fly by an Irish fly-fisher who fishes Lough Sheelin. He told me that it is a common occurrence for the great hatches of buzzer chironomids to mass up in balls on the surface, and that the trout feed well on these larger-than-normal targets as they float helplessly. This artificial represents one of the buzzer masses. I'm told that you shouldn't be without it if you fish Sheelin in early summer.

DRESSING

Hook: Size 10 or 8 long-shank.
Tying silk: Black.
Body hackle: Several long-fibred badger hackles tied in thickly and palmered.
Wings: Several pairs of clear-cut and prepared thick plastic wings tied in at random.
Head: Black varnish.

8 Flash Bang Wallop

COMMENT

This is the pattern which caught the big brown trout from Datchet (Queen Mother Reservoir) which I mentioned in the introduction to this section. The vital statistics bear repetition. The fish weighed 14lb 8oz and is believed to have been stocked at the reservoir as a 2-inch fingerling in 1975. It was 10 years later, on 5 July 1985, that it was caught by David Wood as he was on a pre-match reconnaissance, trying to discover where the shoals of rainbows were feeding. He never did find the rainbow shoals and blanked in the match!

DRESSING

Hook: Size 8 Partridge long-shank.
Tying silk: Black or white.
Tail: Yellow marabou.
Body: Gold Flashabou.
Wing: Four two-inch furnace hackles.
Head: Keep prominent.

Wet Flies

Introduction to Wet Flies

The traditional style of wet-fly fishing which is practised from a broadside-drifting boat has really become popular in the 1980s. The style, which originated on the Scottish lochs and the limestone loughs of Ireland, has a big following on the large reservoirs of England and Wales, where most competitions, both individual and team events, are now fished to International rules. This is a pleasant way of fishing, yet it imposes gentlemanly handicaps. You must not anchor, or use a fly larger than size 10, and you must always cast in front of the drifting boat.

Wet-fly fishing involves using a leader made up with two or three droppers. So when the point-fly is tied on, you are fishing with three (most commonly) or four flies on your cast. The usual practice is to have an attractor/flasher, such as a Butcher or a Dunkeld, on the point and something imitative, such as a Greenwell's Glory, a Blae and Black, a Small Brown Sedge or an Invicta, on the centre dropper or droppers.

For the top dropper, or 'bob-fly', a bushy palmered pattern is the best choice. It can be either imitative (such as a Murrough, a Green Peter or a Black Pennell) for brown trout, or a bright, bushy fly (Old Nick, Orange Muddler, Grenadier or Soldier Palmer) for rainbows in high summer.

Wet-fly fishing is all action, even when few fish are being caught. The style demands continuous short-casting – 5–10 metres is about right in a nice wave – and equally continuous retrieving. A good breeze is necessary if the method is to be practised correctly. Flat calms are greeted with horror by devotees of the style.

It is in a big wave that the bob-fly produces the results. After the short retrieve, the rod is lifted high and held so that the bushy fly dances on the wave-tops for a few seconds. Trout come close to the side of the silently-drifting boat in such conditions, and frequently take just as the bob-fly is lifted off. It is the very opposite, of course, in a flat calm.

To fish loch-style correctly you need a rod at least 10 feet long. Most experts use rods of between 10½ and 12 feet, the latter being the maximum length allowed under International rules.

I've mentioned the Invicta as a good wet-fly pattern, and this is the one I have chosen to describe. It so happens that not only is it a reliable pattern, but it is a fairly complicated one to tie and employs various techniques. So if you can manage this one, you'll have nothing much to worry about with any other wet-fly dressing. It's a rough-looking fly, representing various species of sedge on the point of hatching, and its success confirms one's first impression of it as a good fish-catcher. It is especially useful for loch-style fishing.

The most popular sizes are 10s, 12s, and 14s, so select the one you want – a down-eyed wet-fly hook with a standard shank is the one you need – and put the hook in the vice. If you simply have the bend of the hook in the jaws, you'll find that you have more room in which to work than if you adopt the often-recommended method of completely masking the hook-point. You may have to be a little more careful in seeing that the silk doesn't catch the point, but it's worth while.

The materials you need are: black tying silk; a small topping feather from a golden-pheasant crest for the tail; yellow wool or seal's fur for the body; ribbing of fine round gold tinsel; ginger-brown cock and blue jay hackles; hen-pheasant tail fibres for the wings; and black varnish.

The method is as follows. Catch in the tying silk close to the eye of the hook and wind it back in touching turns towards the bend to make a good firm base for the rest of the materials. Next, catch in the golden-pheasant topping feather at the tail, first straightening out any twist, if necessary, by wetting the feather with water and laying it on a sheet of glass to dry in the required position. Catch it in with three or four turns of tying silk, but don't make the first two too tight. If you do, the feather may twist around the hook-shank. At the same time catch in about three inches of fine round gold tinsel, and then tightly bend down both feather and tinsel towards the eye and trim off the waste.

The body is formed by dubbing (twisting) the strands of seal's fur or wool on to pre-waxed silk and then winding this on to the hook-shank. The silk is waxed to make the dubbed material stick to it. It is as well to take a pinch of seal's fur and rub it in the palm of one hand with the index finger of the other. This mixes the strands in various directions and helps to bind them together. Try to make the dubbed material taper off towards either end of the length of silk, so giving the body slim extremities when the dubbing is wound along the hook-shank. Leave about 2mm of space between the end of the body and the eye of the hook to allow the wing to be tied in.

The next operation is to tie in the body hackle. First strip the soft fluff from the base of the feather, and then tie it in at the eye end of the body with two or three turns of silk. Grip the end of the hackle with hackle-pliers and take it down the shank towards the tail in neat open turns, binding it down (when the correct point is reached) with the gold tinsel which is then wound back towards the eye, trapping the hackle and strengthening the body as a whole. Clip off the waste.

The hook should now be inverted in the vice to enable you to tie in the false hackle of blue jay feather. It is called a false hackle because it is actually formed from a bunch of fibres being tied in rather than from a complete hackle feather being wound on. You achieve this by taking the blue jay feather and tearing a bunch of fibres from it, making sure that the tips are all level. Now trim the bunch to length, this being just greater than the distance between the

eye and the hook-point. Doing this before the fibres are tied in helps to prevent the eye of the hook being obstructed.

Having tied in the false hackle, turn the hook right way up again in the vice ready to take the wing. From each side of the hen-pheasant centre-tail feather tear a slip about ¼-inch wide. Look for a soft, flexible feather with good markings. Make sure that the points are even and lay one slip exactly on top of the other. The wing is now ready to be tied in. This is done by offering the wing up to the hook and tying it in with loops of silk thrown over the wing and drawn tight from below – winging loops, as they are called. These have the effect of pulling the wings straight down on to the hook-shank instead of twisting them. The wing should be just a little longer than the length of the hook, and this should be checked before the silk is finally tightened. Trim off the waste ends of the feather slips, build up a nice neat head with the tying silk, whip-finish and finish it off with a couple of coats of Vycoat. One word of warning about the wings. Do be careful in handling them, because a hen-pheasant tail-feather is prone to split.

The Invicta is just one of the tried-and-tested wet flies which I have included in the section headed 'Sober Wets'. Indeed, many of the flies in the following wet-fly sections have been around long enough to be described as 'traditional', like the method by which they are usually fished.

I have really enjoyed the swing back to popularity of wet-fly fishing. It is never boring, involving more fly-changes in a day than any other method, and I meet lots of new friends in the national competitions. You never know who will be drawn with you to share a boat. Competitions are fished from 10 a.m. until 6 p.m., usually with a good social evening to follow.

Recently England was host to the World Fly Fishing Championships. Twenty-four teams from all over the world, including entries from New Zealand, Australia and America, took part.

Attractor Wets 1

These are all very good point-flies, with the Peach Doll having 'rave reports' in 1985. The Claret Pennell is the dark horse, but, as Terry Oliver will tell you, it's also 'mustard'! I gave Nick Nicholson a few size 12 Cinnamon and Gold, and what did he do with them? He took them on a sea-trout trip to Scotland and then, loch-style drifting with his mentor, Frank Cutler, boated sea trout of 10lb, 9lb 4oz and 6½lb. Frank had caught an eight-pounder earlier in the week, and had told Nick it was the fish of a life-time for a loch-style fisher! Fly-fishing is full of surprises!

1 Teal, Blue and Silver

COMMENT

This is a traditional fly with a fantastic record, not only for luring big trout, but big sea trout as well. It is fished on lochs and reservoirs as a point-fly, where it acts as a flashy attractor. My feeling is that it sometimes attracts trout which then go for the centre or top dropper, normally much more sober flies. This fly takes some beating for sea trout, especially on Welsh rivers. Cyril Inwood favoured it when fishing for, and catching, double-figure specimens on the Conway.

DRESSING

Hook: Size 14, 12, 10 or 8 medium-shank; or larger sizes in tandem as required.
Tying silk: Black.
Tail: Golden-pheasant tippets.
Body: Silver tinsel ribbed with silver wire.
Hackle: Bright blue.
Wing: Teal feather-fibre.
Head: Black varnish.

2 Big Orange

COMMENT

That well-known fly-tyer, Bob Carnill, gave me one of these to try in the 1983 season, having given it a good background report. I first tried it when I was desperate in a flat-calm on Grafham. The occasion was the all-Midland final, and I needed to do well because it was such an important competition. The fly caught me two nice rainbows in the heat of the day in water that was green with algae, and we won the event. This effective wet fly has since helped me in similar circumstances.

DRESSING

Hook: Size 14, 12 or 10.
Tying silk: Olive.
Body: Orange feather-fibre with ribbed gold tinsel.
Hackle: Hot-orange.
Wing: Brown feather-fibre.
Head: Clear varnish.

1 Teal, Blue and Silver **2** Big Orange **3** Brock's Ruby **4** Cinnamon and Gold
5 Teal and Orange **6** Grouse and Red **7** Peach Doll **8** Claret Pennell

3 Brock's Ruby

COMMENT

Sid Brock is one of the best stillwater fly-fishers I know, and he is extremely versatile in his approach. Most of the flies, nymphs and lures he uses are his original tyings. Brock's Ruby takes fish on most waters, but it is at Farmoor I and II that it really catches the rainbows. Red has become a fashionable colour since the success of the Nailer Fly.

DRESSING

Hook: Size 10, 8 or 6 long-shank bronze.
Tying silk: Black.
Tail: Bright red long cock or hen hackle-fibres.
Body: Red floss underbody covered in stretched clear polythene.
Hackle: Orange hackle-fibres. Throat only.
Cheeks: Golden-pheasant tippet.
Wing: Four red cock hackles.
Head: Black varnish.

4 Cinnamon and Gold

COMMENT

This is a traditional wet-fly pattern which imitates various members of the sedge family. Its value is that it can be fished fast in the surface film. Trout feeding selectively can be difficult to tempt, but they seem to go for this fly better than others when it is retrieved quickly, and a fast retrieve also gives it a good hooking ratio. Cast at rising fish on the upwind side, and then quickly pull the fly away from them.

DRESSING

Hook: Size 14, 12 or 10 medium-shank bronze.
Tying silk: Black.
Tail: None.
Body: Gold tinsel.
Hackle: Light brown cock.
Wing: Brown feather-fibre, paired as in all wet flies.
Head: Black varnish.

5 Teal and Orange

COMMENT

The teal series of winged wet flies are all tied in the same way, the only variation being the colour. This one is a favourite of mine, especially in high summer when plenty of super-fit rainbows are in the reservoirs. I use it as a point-fly when fishing from a boat in traditional style – short-lining with a floating line. One evening at Ravensthorpe, when trout were rising to sedges yet were difficult to tempt, I tore the wing from a Teal and Orange to give myself an orange-and-olive nymph. Those same trout were soon virtually queuing up to take it!

DRESSING

Hook: Size 14, 12 or 10 medium-shank bronze.
Tying silk: Black.
Tail: A few strands of golden-pheasant tippet.
Body: Orange seal's fur or wool ribbed with fine, gold oval thread.
Hackle: Medium-olive.
Wing: Spray of fibres from the breast of a teal.
Head: Black varnish.

6 Grouse and Red

COMMENT

It is in Scotland that other grousewing body colours are most used, and they are favourites for traditional loch-style fishing. This red-bodied version is becoming popular on the English reservoirs in the wake of enthusiasm which competitive fishing has created for this style. Fish the Grouse and Red on the point of a team of three wet flies.

DRESSING

Hook: Size 14, 12 or 10.
Tying silk: Black or red.
Tail: Golden-pheasant tippets.
Body: Red seal's fur or wool ribbed with silver wire.
Hackle: Red cock.
Wing: Grouse feather-fibre.
Head: Black or clear varnish.

7 Peach Doll

COMMENT

What a sensation this pattern caused during the 1984 and 1985 seasons! Bob Morey introduced me to it in June 1984, and I had some amazing results with it while surface fishing. The secret of using it successfully is that you must be brave enough to take it off if you are having follow after follow, but no hooked trout to show for your efforts. At other times you may have eight offers and eight fish landed in little more than an hour. Bob Morey took the record Benson and Hedges specimen, a brown of 7lb 6oz from Grafham, on this fly in June 1985.

DRESSING

Hook: Size 12 or 10.
Tying silk: Black.
Tail and back: Peach-coloured nylon wool. Keep the tail prominent and fluffy after trimming.
Body: Peach-coloured nylon wool.
Head: Black varnish.

8 Claret Pennell

COMMENT

I found a batch of these flies in a 'job lot' I purchased, and couldn't but notice how interesting they looked. The Black Pennell is good, I reasoned, and claret is a killing colour in other patterns. So I bet these will work. They did – on Rutland, especially, and on Grafham. I had three or four good catches on the pattern used as a top dropper. Then I gave a couple to England International Terry Oliver. He has since favoured the fly after regular good catches.

DRESSING

Hook: Size 14, 12 or 10.
Tying silk: Black.
Tail: Golden-pheasant tippets.
Body: Claret seal's fur or wool ribbed with silver wire.
Hackle: Black hen, wound generously.
Head: Black varnish.

Attractor Wets 2

These excellent point-flies should be used and changed regularly until the best pattern of the day is found. Dunkeld and Butcher are two of my favourites, and a Silver March Brown can sometimes work wonders. The Wickham's and Silver Invicta are good in the summer months. All are useful patterns on the big reservoirs, with boat fishing giving the best results.

1   Silver March Brown

COMMENT

The March Brown and Silver March Brown date back almost 250 years. The fact that the Silver March Brown hardly looks like the fly which actually hatches in the rough, rocky rivers of the North doesn't seem to matter. What does matter is that it is a proven and deadly wet-fly pattern which seems to work everywhere, especially early in the season. Skues once said of it: 'It is an excellent fly, although quite a poor imitation of the natural, but passable for almost anything else.' That sums it up!

DRESSING

Hook: Size 14, 12 or 10 medium-shank bronze.
Tying silk: Black.
Tail: A few strands of partridge hackle.
Body: Silver tinsel ribbed with fine silver wire.
Hackle: Dark brown hen or, as a variant, fine light partridge. Beard only.
Wing: Hen pheasant.
Head: Black varnish.

2   Dunkeld Wet Fly

COMMENT

The Dunkeld wet fly has again proved a popular and deadly pattern since traditional loch-style fishing has made such a comeback. Fish it on the point, where its qualities of attraction will move fish on the dourest of days. It originates from a variation of the famous salmon fly of the same name.

DRESSING

Hook: Size 14, 12 or 10.
Tying silk: Black.
Tail: Golden-pheasant crest.
Body: Flat gold tinsel ribbed with gold wire.
Hackle: Hot-orange cock fibres; throat only or palmered.
Wing: Bronze mallard.
Eyes: This fly works well with jungle cock or jungle cock substitute eyes.
Head: Black varnish.

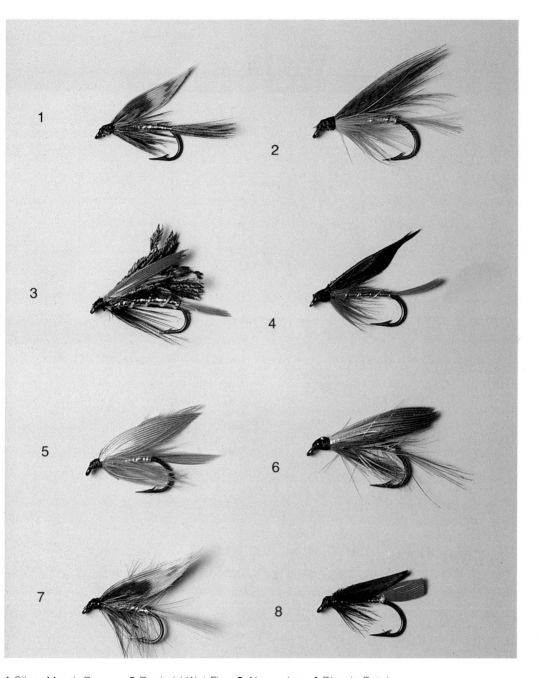

1 Silver March Brown   **2** Dunkeld Wet Fly   **3** Alexandra   **4** Bloody Butcher
5 Hardy's Gold Butcher   **6** Wickham's Fancy   **7** Silver Invicta   **8** Butcher

3 Alexandra

COMMENT

The Alexandra is a traditional pattern which was known originally as The Lady of the Lake and renamed around 1860 in honour of Queen Alexandra. It can be used in small sizes as a wet fly or in large sizes as a lure. The larger type of fly used to be known as a 'Demon'. This is without doubt purely an attractor pattern which arouses the aggressive instincts of trout. I know one fly-fisher who uses this pattern almost exclusively when he is fishing for sea trout.

DRESSING

Hook: Size 14, 12 or 10 bronze for a wet fly; size 8 or 6 bronze for a tandem lure.
Tying silk: Black.
Tail: Red ibis feather or golden-pheasant crest fibres.
Body: Flat silver tinsel.
Hackle: Black hen.
Wings: Strands of green peacock herl with cheeks of red ibis or golden-pheasant crest.
Head: Black varnish.

4 Bloody Butcher

COMMENT

This was one of the first flies I ever used in my early fly-fishing days at Ravensthorpe. I didn't catch many trout, because Ravensthorpe then received a stocking of only 2,000 trout a year. However, I used it with great success at neighbouring Pitsford in the early 1960s. Sometimes I would fish it deep and slow along the bottom after allowing my silk line to become water-logged, so that I could use it as a sinker. Really, I was using the fly as a mini-lure. The red throat hackle often seems to make all the difference between catching and not catching.

DRESSING

Hook: Size 14, 12 or 10.
Tying silk: Black.
Tail: Red feather-fibre.
Body: Silver tinsel ribbed with silver wire.
Hackle: Bright red cock.
Wing: Blue mallard wing feather or crow substitute.
Head: Black varnish.

5 Hardy's Gold Butcher

COMMENT

This is an excellent point-fly for traditional loch-style fishing in Scotland and on English and Welsh reservoirs. It sometimes kills well when its cousins, the Butcher, Bloody Butcher and Dunkeld, fail. It is difficult to understand why this should be, yet I have known it to happen on a number of occasions.

DRESSING

Hook: Size 14, 12 or 10.
Tying silk: Black.
Tail: Blue feather-fibre.
Body: Gold tinsel ribbed with gold wire.
Hackle: Hot-orange cock.
Wing: Lightest grey starling.
Head: Black varnish.

6 Wickham's Fancy

COMMENT

This is one of my favourite summer wet flies, and one which has given me many good catches over the years. It is an old-established fly which many anglers use when fishing loch-style. It fishes well when sedges are about. I use it as a point-fly on a floating line and vary the hook-size according to the wind strength – the bigger the wave, the bigger the hook.

DRESSING

Hook: Size 14, 12 or 10 medium-shank bronze.
Tying silk: Black.
Tail: A few fibres of ginger cock hackle.
Body: Flat gold tinsel ribbed with fine gold wire.
Ribbing Hackle: Ginger cock.
Hackle: Ginger cock.
Wing: Medium starling.
Head: Black varnish.

7 Silver Invicta

COMMENT

This fly is at its best as summer wears on. It fishes well when used on a floating line in June, July and August. If sedges are about, so much the better. Fish the fly loch-style and fish will rise to it. Cover fish that rise slightly upwind and they will also take.

DRESSING

Hook: Size 14, 12 or 10 medium-shank bronze.
Tying silk: Black.
Tail: Golden-pheasant crest whisks.
Body: Silver tinsel ribbed with ginger-brown cock hackle tied palmer-style.
Wing: Hen-pheasant feather.
Hackle: A few fibres of blue jay.
Head: Black varnish.

8 Butcher

COMMENT

This is perhaps the best-known of all wet flies. It dates back more than 150 years and was named after a Kent family-butcher whose name was Mr Moon. It was devised by a Mr Jewhurst, one of his customers. Many anglers have great faith in this pattern even today. It scores best as a point-fly on a team of three fished loch-style. I have also used it to good effect on a slow-sink shooting-head, making a long cast and retrieving the fly steadily along the bottom.

DRESSING

Hook: Size 14, 12 or 10. Some anglers use 8s or 6s for sea trout.
Tying silk: Black.
Tail: Red Ibis.
Body: Flat silver ribbed with oval silver.
Hackle: Black.
Wing: Blue-black feather from a drake's wing.
Head: Black varnish.

Deceiver Wets 1

These are excellent traditional patterns for loch-style wet-fly fishing from a drifting boat. I would fish most of them on the centre dropper, or perhaps on the point. The Black Pennell would be the exception, to be used occasionally on the bob. The Black Pennell and Blae and Black cover early-season needs when the small black chironomid is on the water, with the Olive and Ginger Quills coming into their own in early summer. These flies work on all waters of size, be they reservoir, loch or lough.

1   Ginger Quill

COMMENT

This is one of the best imitative patterns, and a brilliant fly on a size 14 hook at Eyebrook during July and August evenings. In 1985 I took a limit from Draycote of 16½lb in a short morning session while using a size 12 Ginger Quill on my point. Fish were rising and I fished the fly slowly through the steady ripple.

DRESSING

Hook: Size 14, 12 or 10.
Tying silk: Black.
Tail: Ginger cock hackle-fibres.
Body: Peacock quill dyed ginger.
Wing: Pale starling.
Hackle: Ginger cock.
Head: Black varnish.

2   Teal and Black

COMMENT

This fly came to my notice as something special many years ago during my first trip to Lough Mask. Paul Harris was with me and it was early May. Black chironomids were still hatching (the Irish call them duckflies) and Paul caught virtually all his fish on this pattern. It's certainly one to try early in the season.

DRESSING

Hook: Size 14, 12 or 10.
Tying silk: Black.
Tail: Golden-pheasant tippets.
Body: Black seal's fur ribbed with silver wire.
Hackle: Black hen.
Wing: Well-marked teal feather.
Head: Black varnish.

1 Ginger Quill 2 Teal and Black 3 Olive Quill 4 Alder Fly
5 Blae and Black 6 Coachman 7 Grouse and Green 8 Black Pennell

3 Olive Quill

COMMENT

Olive and ginger chironomids are common at Chew Valley, where they seem to be larger than on other waters. I have taken some nice fish on the Olive Quill, and its close relation the Ginger Quill, when boat-fishing there on an ideal day with the occasional fish rising to these buzzers.

DRESSING

Hook: Size 14, 12 or 10 medium-shank bronze.
Tying silk: Black, green or brown.
Tail: Olive cock hackle fibres.
Body: Stripped peacock herl dyed olive.
Hackle: Olive cock.
Wing: Starling or grey substitute.
Head: Black or clear varnish.

4 Alder Fly

COMMENT

It seems generally agreed that trout don't eat the common early-season alder flies which can be seen hatching in their hundreds. An alder fly would make quite a large mouthful, yet trout caught and spooned do not show this fly in their stomachs. However, the artificial Alder catches trout quite well in midsummer, when I believe it is taken as a dark sedge.

DRESSING

Hook: Size 14, 12 or 10.
Tying silk: Black.
Body: Bronze peacock herl.
Hackle: Black hen.
Wing: Mottled-brown feather-fibre.
Head: Black varnish.

5 Blae and Black

COMMENT

One of my great heroes was that expert fisherman Cyril Inwood. He used this fly a lot, especially in April and May when small black chironomids were hatching at most reservoirs. The fly is usually fished on the point of a team of three. A size 14 is best in a light breeze, a size 12 in a six-inch wave, and a size 10 in anything bigger. Fish it in traditional style from a boat, or from a headland on the bank.

DRESSING

Hook: Size 14, 12 or 10.
Tying silk: Black.
Tail: Golden-pheasant tippets.
Body: Black floss ribbed with silver wire.
Hackle: Black hen.
Wing: Medium-grey starling.
Head: Black varnish.

6 Coachman

COMMENT

This old English pattern was devised by a coachman to the Royal Family. Although this dressing is for the wet version, it is perhaps best known as a dry fly (*see* page 225). I use this wet pattern with confidence at sedge time, and it scores well during daytime when fished on or close to the surface.

DRESSING

Hook: Size 14, 12 or 10.
Tying silk: Black.
Body: Bronze peacock herl.
Wing: White duck.
Hackle: Natural medium-brown cock.
Head: Black varnish.

7 Grouse and Green

COMMENT

This fly is a great favourite in Scotland. In many ways it is similar to the Irish Sooty Olive. I rather neglect this fly myself, yet I hear of many good catches on it. The grousewing series includes other colours, and orange, claret, grey and red are recommended.

DRESSING

Hook: Size 14, 12 or 10.
Tying silk: Black.
Body: Green seal's fur or substitute ribbed with fine silver tinsel.
Hackle: Ginger hen.
Wing: Grouse feather-fibres.
Head: Black varnish.

8 Black Pennell

COMMENT

The Black Pennell is a great early-season fly, and like the Black and Peacock Spider, it is very versatile. It was devised many years ago by H. Cholmondely-Pennell, who was also responsible for hook-designs which are still in use today. The largest fish I saw caught on this fly were a brace of 7lb-plus rainbows.

DRESSING

Hook: Size 14, 12, 10 or 8 medium-shank bronze.
Tying silk: Black.
Tail: Golden-pheasant tippet fibres.
Body: Slim black floss silk ribbed with fine, oval silver wire.
Hackle: Long-fibred black cock. Make two or three full turns.
Head: Black varnish.

Deceiver Wets 2

Some of this set are flies of similar family and I like all except one. The Black and Peacock Spider is a fly I use regularly at the start of the season. Fished slowly and deep-down on a sinking line, it works every time. I also have great faith in the Zulu, but little in the Blue Zulu which just doesn't catch fish for me, although I still fish it from time to time.

1 Ke-He

COMMENT

This fly was devised by a Mr Kemp and a Mr Heddle when they were fishing the famous Loch of Harray in the Orkney Islands, and it takes its name from their names. The Ke-He was supposed to represent a small dark bee that fell in great numbers on the Loch's surface, blown there by the wind. The fly is still a great Scottish favourite, and is used as a general pattern on many lochs. One angler I know ties his Ke-Hes with an especially bushy hackle and always fishes them on the bob.

DRESSING

Hook: 14, 12 or 10.
Tying silk: Black.
Tails: Golden-pheasant tippet and a snippet of red wool.
Body: Bronze peacock herl.
Hackle: Medium-brown cock.
Head: Black varnish.

2 Blue Zulu

COMMENT

Blue is not often used in modern patterns, and it is for this reason that I give this old-timer an occasional wetting. I'm told it can be useful during summer when a big wind is blowing, although it does not work well for me. It is a fancy pattern, used purely as an attractor.

DRESSING

Hook: Size 8, 10, 12 or 14 medium-shank bronze.
Tying silk: Black.
Tail: Short section of red wool.
Body: Black wool or seal's fur ribbed with fine, flat silver tinsel.
Hackle: Three turns of long-fibred cock dyed blue and tied just behind the head and a black palmered body hackle.
Head: Black varnish.

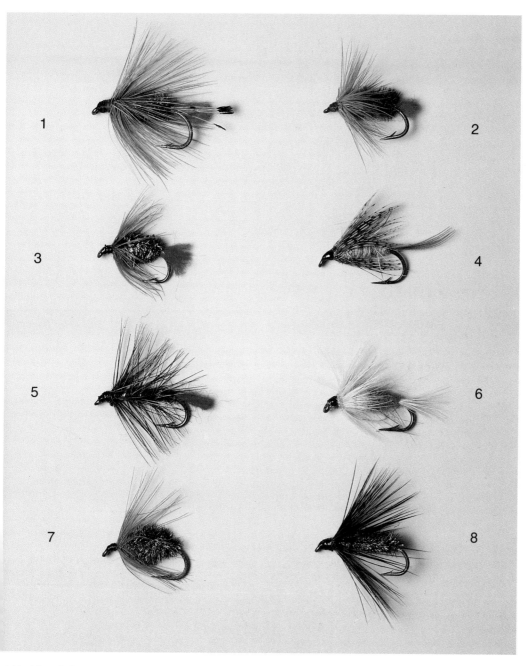

1 Ke-He **2** Blue Zulu **3** Red Tag **4** March Brown Spider
5 Zulu **6** Brown and Yellow Sedge **7** Green and Peacock Spider
8 Black and Peacock Spider

3 Red Tag

COMMENT

In the past the Red Tag has been considered primarily a river fly – and a grayling pattern at that. Its coloration is similar to that of a Wormfly, a pattern which does well early in the season when fished deep-down on the reservoirs. Now the Red Tag has a growing reputation as a top or centre dropper, and it is one of the favourite flies that English International Terry Oliver has on his cast when he fishes at Rutland Water.

DRESSING

Hook: Size 14, 12 or 10.
Tying silk: Black.
Tail: Bright red wool.
Body: Bronze and green peacock herl mixed.
Hackle: Ginger brown cock.
Head: Black varnish.

4 March Brown Spider

COMMENT

This pattern is a good one on the spate rivers of the North and Wales, where the fly is common in March and April. It is best fished on a floating line cast across the stream and allowed to come round naturally with the current. The fly is also used on stillwaters as a general pattern, and there is no doubt that it works quite well.

DRESSING

Hook: Size 14, 12 or 10.
Tying silk: Black.
Tail: Brown feather-fibre.
Body: Grey rabbit or brown dubbing mix ribbed with silver wire.
Hackle: Silver-brown speckled partridge hackle.
Head: Black varnish.

5 Zulu

COMMENT

I have used this extremely good pattern since the first day I went fly-fishing. It was successful then and I still use it regularly and successfully. It has great versatility, it can be fished deep as a small lure in the early season, and later on as a bob-fly fished back through the waves. This is definitely one of my great favourites.

DRESSING

Hook: Size 14, 12 or 10.
Tying silk: Black.
Tail: Scarlet wool.
Body: Black wool or seal's fur ribbed with fine, flat silver tinsel.
Body hackle: Palmered black cock.
Head: Black varnish.

6 Brown and Yellow Sedge

COMMENT

This is an amazing pattern. It can be fished slowly through the surface area during a sedge hatch, or it can be dressed with a lead or copper-wire underbody and fished as a point-fly along the bottom. It does well in either position. I assume it is taken for a sedge pupa at the top and a caddis grub larva deep-down. I recommend that you tie some in each style.

DRESSING

Hook: Size 12 or 10 long-shank.
Tying silk: Black.
Tail: Yellow hackle-fibres.
Body: Rear half, brown seal's fur or dubbing mix, or peacock herl; front half, yellow seal's fur or dubbing mix ribbed with fine gold wire.
Hackle: Yellow hen.
Head: Black varnish.

7 Green and Peacock Spider

COMMENT

Tom Iven's Black and Peacock Spider is well known and has landed thousands of trout for thousands of anglers, so it is little wonder that this first-cousin is also a very good fly. When Godfrey Hudson asked me to try it out, I put it in my box and it stayed there until one day on Rutland. I tied it on and had three quick trout between 4.30 p.m. and 5.15 p.m. when I had to pack up. It would seem to work when fished similarly to the style recommended for the original.

DRESSING

Hook: Size 14, 12 or 10.
Tying silk: Black.
Body: Bronze peacock herl.
Hackle: Green hen.
Head: Black varnish.

8 Black and Peacock Spider

COMMENT

This old favourite was popularised by Tom Ivens just after the Second World War. It is a great deceiver and can be fished either high in the water as a bob-fly, making a wake in a big wave, or on a sinking shooting head as a bottom-grubber.

DRESSING

Hook: Size 14, 12 or 10 medium-shank bronze.
Tying silk: Black.
Tail: None.
Body: Bronze peacock herl reinforced with a reverse-wound ribbing of fuse wire.
Hackle: Three or four full turns of long-fibred hen.
Head: Black varnish.

Sober Wets

In this selection we have some of the all-time greats. Who would be without an Invicta, a Claret Sedge, a Greenwell's Glory or a Fiery Brown? No one, of course, because they are such proven patterns, taking browns or rainbows in reservoir or loch with great consistency. A pattern I am particularly pleased with is the June Fly, one of my own tyings. It often out-fishes the famous Greenwell's Glory on waters where olives abound.

1 Winged Hare's Ear

COMMENT

This is an excellent but little-used wet fly. Nearly every fly-fisher knows and uses the Gold-ribbed Hare's Ear Nymph, but not many try this wet fly. It looks very much like a newly-hatched chironomid or small sedge. As these are the two most common flies hatching and being eaten by trout in a British summer, take my tip and give this one a trial.

DRESSING

Hook: Size 14, 12 or 10.
Tying silk: Black.
Tail: Ginger cock hackle-fibres.
Body: Hare's ear or face fur dubbed on and ribbed with silver wire.
Hackle: Ginger cock.
Wing: Light grey starling.
Head: Black varnish.

2 Claret Sedge

COMMENT

Bearing some similarity to the Claret and Mallard and Claret Murrough, the Claret Sedge just has to catch trout. I use it as a general wet-fly pattern and find it works quite well throughout the season on all large waters.

DRESSING

Hook: Size 14, 12 or 10.
Tying silk: Black.
Tail: Golden-pheasant tippets.
Body: Claret Superla dubbing ribbed with silver wire.
Hackle: Black or claret hen.
Wing: A prominent wing of dark brown feather-fibre.
Head: Black varnish.

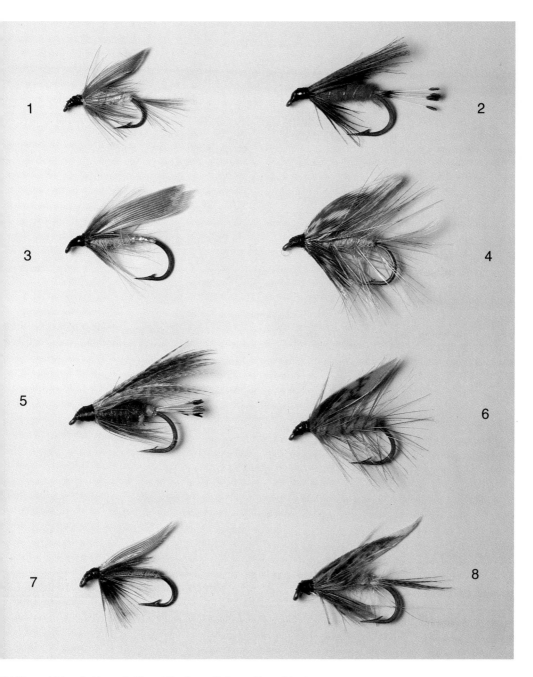

1 Winged Hare's Ear **2** Claret Sedge **3** June Fly **4** Invicta
5 Fiery Brown **6** Small Brown Sedge **7** Greenwell's Glory **8** March Brown

3 June Fly

COMMENT

From mid-May until the end of June, Pitsford is alive with fly-life on most days suitable for a hatch. These hatches are always of dark olive chironomids and pond olives. I devised the June Fly especially for Pitsford at this time of year. To say it is excellent is an understatement – it has beaten all other flies quite easily. Fish it on a floating line.

DRESSING

Hook: Size 14, 12 or 10.
Tying silk: Black or olive.
Tag: Gold Lurex tied round the hook-bend.
Body: Pale pastel-green or olive wool.
Hackle: Furnace.
Wing: Starling or grey substitute.
Head: Black varnish with black tying silk, clear with olive.

4 Invicta

COMMENT

Trout on most waters soon develop a taste for sedges when these start to hatch. The Invicta is a good artificial which imitates the hatching or adult fly. I have caught several good fish, browns and rainbows, off the top while using it during the evening at Rutland. I always use a floating line with this pattern and I retrieve the fly slowly on or just below the surface. Drifting loch-style is probably the best method to adopt.

DRESSING

Hook: Size 14, 12 or 10 medium-shank bronze.
Tying silk: Black.
Tail: Golden-pheasant crest.
Body: Yellow wool or seal's fur ribbed with fine, round gold wire and with a ginger-brown cock body hackle.
Hackle: Ginger-brown and blue jay.
Wing: Hen-pheasant tail fibre.
Head: Black varnish.

5 Fiery Brown (variant)

COMMENT

I include this variant of the Fiery Brown simply because it works best of all in small sizes. It is a good pattern to try in sizes 16 and 14 when a few fish are rising regularly in crystal-clear water. At such times I scale down my leader and use a 3lb breaking-strain tip – and I refrain from casting repeatedly.

DRESSING

Hook: Size 16, 14 or 12.
Tying silk: Black.
Tail: Golden-pheasant tippets.
Tag: Orange floss.
Body: Dark brown wool ribbed with gold wire.
Hackle: Dark brown.
Head: Black varnish.

6 Small Brown Sedge

COMMENT

I began to use this pattern often as my interest in surface loch-style fishing increased from 1980 onwards. It is regularly on my cast on any of the English reservoirs from late June through to September. It is such a good imitative sedge pattern that I frequently put it on the centre dropper, which is perhaps the least-effective fly position. Not so with this fly. It is highly recommended.

DRESSING

Hook: Size 14, 12 or 10.
Tying silk: Black.
Body: Brown Superla dubbing or Antron ribbed with gold wire.
Body Hackle: Medium-brown cock, palmered.
Wing: Medium-brown feather-fibre.
Head: Black varnish.

7 Greenwell's Glory

COMMENT

The Greenwell's Glory is one of the best-known and most respected imitative wet-fly patterns. It has accounted for countless thousands of trout since it was first used by Canon William Greenwell in May 1854. Modern trout-fishers often fish it in the surface film when fish are feeding on various olive-coloured flies. Dry-fly and nymph versions, of similar coloration, complete a set to suit all conditions when olive or green flies are about from May onwards on stillwaters or rivers.

DRESSING

Hook: Size 16, 14, 12, 10 or 8 medium-shank bronze.
Tying silk: Dull yellow.
Tail: Furnace cock hackle-fibres.
Body: Yellow tying silk waxed to give olive effect in water and ribbed with fine gold tinsel thread.
Hackle: Two turns of furnace.
Wing: The original was from the inside of a blackbird's wing. Starling is a good substitute.
Head: Clear varnish.

8 March Brown

COMMENT

This sober-coloured imitative wet fly is one of the best deceiver patterns, particularly at Tittesworth where I have had great sport on it during hatches of small buzzers.

DRESSING

Hook: Size 14, 12 or 10.
Tying silk: Brown.
Tail: Light partridge hackle whisks.
Body: Grey rabbit or seal's fur ribbed with gold wire.
Hackle: Dark partridge.
Wing: Hen pheasant.
Head: Clear varnish.

Bob-flies

This selection includes some fine top-dropper 'bob-flies'. I discovered the American Queen of the Water pattern several years ago and I have often done well with it. The Bumbles are best kept for big-wave conditions. The famous Chew Valley Grenadier has become a top favourite on the big Midlands reservoirs as well and is fast approaching the Soldier Palmer in the popularity ratings. The trout must surely take it to be an emerging buzzer struggling from its skin to become an adult winged fly. The rest of the collection are good top droppers.

1   Great Red Sedge

COMMENT

Many dressings of this large sedge have been handed down over the years. This is one I devised in Ireland, when the Grey Murrough artificial was doing well on Mask and I decided I could better the local dressing. It caught well for me on Mask, Carra and Conn in sizes 10 and 8. However, it was when I tied some size 14 and 12 versions that I had my best sport. This can be used as a normal sedge pattern when the grousewings and silverhorns are on the reservoirs in July and August.

DRESSING

Hook: Size 14, 12, 10 or 8.
Tying silk: Black.
Tail: Dark brown cock hackle-fibres.
Body: Dark grey rabbit fur dubbed on and ribbed with fine gold wire.
Body hackle: Dark brown cock, palmered.
Wing: Hen pheasant or grouse.
Head: Black varnish.

2   Chew Emerger

COMMENT

This fly is tied on one of the new specially-shaped Emerger hooks. The pattern causes plenty of disturbance when it is fished through the waves. At the end of the retrieve, during the all-important 'pause' or 'bobbing' of the fly, any following fish hopefully sees the body-shape of an insect breaking from its nymphal shuck – a stage at which trout seem especially to like to take a nymph. The up-eyed hook allows the fly to hang in the surface at just the right angle. It's a must!

DRESSING

Hook: Size 14, 12 or 10 up-eyed with curved shank.
Tying silk: Black.
Tag: Pearl Flashabou.
Body: Rusty-orange seal's fur ribbed with fine gold oval tinsel.
Body Hackle: Honey cock, palmered.
Thorax: Medium-brown seal's fur or wool.
Wing: Cree cock hackle-tips.
Head: Black varnish.

1 Great Red Sedge   **2** Chew Emerger   **3** Silver Zulu   **4** Olive Bumble
5 Grasshopper   **6** Grenadier   **7** Queen of the Water   **8** Claret Bumble

3 Silver Zulu

COMMENT

This alternative to the black-bodied Zulu is a good top dropper in winds of average strength and a good point-fly in very strong winds and a high wave. It is useful at any time of the season, but especially so in the early and late stages; in April, for example, when a lot of black flies are showing on most large waters, and in October, when with falling water temperatures, black again becomes good.

DRESSING

Hook: Size 14, 12, 10 or 8.
Tying silk: Black.
Tail: Fluorescent red floss.
Body: Silver tinsel ribbed with silver wire.
Body Hackle: Black hen.
Head hackle: Black cock.
Head: Black varnish.

4 Olive Bumble

COMMENT

Irish fly-fisher and author T.C. Kingsmill-Moore devised this fly. Robbie O'Grady gave me one to try when I was out with him on Lough Mask. He rates it a great pattern in a big wind, because it makes a good wake even when the wave is high. Robbie should know – he is the only man to have won the World Wet-fly Championships (held on Mask each August) on two occasions. A recommended pattern.

DRESSING

Hook: Size 12, 10 or 8.
Tying silk: Olive.
Body: Olive and brown seal's fur mixed ribbed with fine gold oval tinsel.
Body hackles: Golden-olive and light brown, palmered.
Head hackle: Guinea-fowl dyed blue.
Head: Clear varnish.

5 Grasshopper

COMMENT

Dapping the natural grasshopper is probably the most deadly surface-fishing method for catching sizeable wild browns on the big Irish Loughs from mid to late summer. I often wonder why we don't try the method more on our large English reservoirs. It was only to be expected that a good Irish artificial Grasshopper would be available in a tackle-shop near Lough Mask, so I bought one and did catch a couple of trout with it on the point while wet-fly fishing in a high wave.

DRESSING

Hook: Size 10 or 8.
Tying silk: Black.
Body: White floss ribbed with silver wire.
Underwing: Yellow feather-fibre.
Overwing: Olive feather-fibre.
Legs: Knotted bronze peacock herl.
Hackle: Olive cock, wound prominently.
Head: Black varnish.

6 Grenadier

COMMENT

Top-class fly-fishers from the Bristol area – such as Chris Ogborne, Steve Pope and John Braithwaite – have favoured the Grenadier for many years. Not only do they regularly win competitions with it at Chew Valley, but they more than hold their own when they fish against their great Midlands rivals at Rutland and Grafham. The fly has a few variations. It is used for traditional fishing either palmered as a top dropper, or not palmered as a point-fly.

DRESSING

Hook: Size 14, 12 or 10.
Tying silk: Brown.
Body: Orange seal's fur ribbed with gold wire.
Body hackle: Ginger cock, palmered.
Head hackle: Ginger cock.
Head: Clear varnish.

7 Queen of the Water

COMMENT

This is one of the best top dropper flies I know. It is of American origin. I remember trying it at Rutland during the Pro-Am competition in June 1981. It was a day of bright sun and light ripple and fish were generally hard to come by. I fished the Queen of the Water quite fast on the top dropper and caught nine rainbows on it to win the event comfortably. Since then, backed by my confidence in the fly, it has given me many more similar good bags at Rutland and Grafham.

DRESSING

Hook: Size 14, 12 or 10.
Tying silk: Black.
Tail: Bright red or brown cock hackle-fibres.
Body: Drab-orange floss.
Body hackle: Brown cock, palmered.
Wing: Teal.
Head: Black varnish.

8 Claret Bumble

COMMENT

This was another present from Robbie O'Grady, and it has become my favourite Bumble pattern. Bumble is simply another description of a palmered fly, and the name dates back more than 200 years. Claret seems particularly attractive to wild brown trout – witness the success of the Claret and Mallard, the Claret Murrough, the Claret Pennell and the Claret Nymph. These flies and the Claret Bumble often tempt wild browns far better than any other colour fly when fished on or close to the surface.

DRESSING

Hook: Size 12, 10 or 8.
Tying silk: Black.
Tail: Golden-pheasant tippets.
Body: Claret seal's fur ribbed with gold fine oval tinsel.
Body hackle: Claret cock, palmered.
Head hackle: Guinea-fowl dyed blue.
Head: Black varnish.

Sedges

The bottom-crawling and ascending-pupa patterns given in this section allow you to make up a good three-fly cast when the sedges are up and the conditions right on July and August evenings. At this time the big Midlands reservoirs are particularly good from the bank. One angler might fish all day and go home blank at 7 p.m., whereas another might arrive to have just two hours' fishing and catch several fish and see them rising all evening. The cream of the hatches come in the last two weeks of July and the first two of August. The flies hatch in calm, shallow water as the light fades, and it is then that fish come close inshore to feed on them.

1 Green-arsed Sedge

COMMENT

One of the top rods on Pitsford is the experienced Hector Woolnough. He is a fine fly-fisherman who uses the dry fly in preference to all other methods, and he has devised quite a few new patterns. This one, (with apologies for its name) is the most deadly and most famous. It should be sprayed with silicone and fished proud on top. Fishing the fly static regularly brings the best results. It can be used as a wake fly when necessary.

DRESSING

Hook: Size 14, 12 or 10.
Tying silk: Black.
Tail and Body: Fluffy green nylon wool.
Hackle: Light ginger cock.
Head: Black varnish.

2 Ombudsman

COMMENT

This is Brian Clarke's well-known version of the caddis larva. Brian likes to fish with longer-than-normal leaders, a method he has often recommended. This is the way to fish this fly, using a floating fly-line and a slow retrieve.

DRESSING

Hook: Size 10 or 8 long-shank leaded beneath the body or weighted with copper wire.
Tying silk: Red.
Tail: Fluorescent lime-green wool.
Body: Bronze peacock herl ribbed with copper wire.
Wing: Brown-mottled feather.
Hackle: Dark brown hen.
Head: Clear varnish.

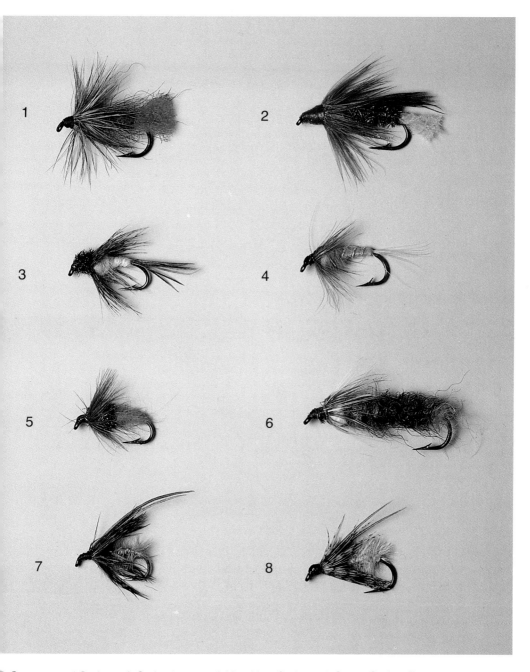

1 Green-arsed Sedge   2 Ombudsman   3 Hatching Sedge   4 Green Sedge Pupa
5 Green and Brown Sedge Pupa   6 Cave's Caddis Larva   7 Green Longhorn
8 Amber Longhorn

3 Hatching Sedge

COMMENT

Sedges, in their various stages, form an important part of a trout's diet. We can imitate the insect in its larval, pupal, or adult stage of life. This dressing is just one of many hatching patterns. It works well when fished on a floating fly-line, with best results usually achieved in the two hours before dusk.

DRESSING

Hook: Size 14, 12 or 10 medium-shank bronze.
Tying silk: Black.
Tail: Pheasant-tail fibres.
Body: White wool ribbed with fine oval silver tinsel.
Thorax: Amber or yellow seal's fur dubbed on. Leave in a few pheasant-tail fibres to make a shellback finish.
Hackle: One turn of brown hen.
Head: One strand of peacock herl tied in close to the hook-eye.

4 Green Sedge Pupa

COMMENT

This is another pupa pattern which fishes best close to the surface. It is essentially a pattern for July and August when sedges are at their thickest, and is not worth bothering with unless they are hatching quite well, except that it can be useful in a rise of pond olives.

DRESSING

Hook: Size 14, 12 or 10.
Tying silk: Black.
Tail: White cock hackle-fibres.
Body: Bright green wool ribbed with fine silver oval tinsel.
Thorax: Olive seal's fur.
Hackle: Medium-brown hen.
Head: Black varnish.

5 Green and Brown Sedge Pupa

COMMENT

Pitsford regular Vic Wright invented this pattern to be used during this reservoir's tremendous sedge hatches. The pupa has a reputation for tempting the big fish to take, and browns of more than 5lb have been caught on it. Use it in July and August for the best results. The pattern has been proved on other waters as well, mostly Midlands reservoirs.

DRESSING

Hook: Size 14, 12 or 10.
Tying silk: Black.
Body: Bright green seal's fur.
Thorax: Bronze peacock herl.
Hackle: Ginger hen.
Head: Black varnish.

6 Cave's Caddis Larva

COMMENT

Herbie Cave gave me a set of his neat and realistic-looking caddis larvae imitations, but it was some time before I used them. However, when I did I caught some quality trout by fishing slow and deep. The first occasion was at Churn Pool in Gloucestershire. Later the pattern was successful at Ringstead and Grafham. It is easy to tie, as I discovered when I needed to replace Herbie's by tying a few of my own.

DRESSING

Hook: Size 10 or 8 long-shank.
Tying silk: Black.
Body: A mixture of amber, black and olive long-fibred wool unwound, dubbed on and ribbed with copper wire.
Thorax: White wool.
Hackle: Badger hen.
Head: Black varnish.

7 Green Longhorn

COMMENT

Richard Walker always reckoned that this green version of his Longhorn worked best during late May or early June when few sedges were about. I have used it when green mayfly have been hatching on various waters. I imagine it is taken for the mayfly nymph which is about to hatch. At such times, it should be fished just below the surface.

DRESSING

Hook: Size 14, 12 or 10.
Tying silk: Black.
Body: Olive-green ostrich herl ribbed with silver wire.
Thorax: Black ostrich herl.
Hackle: Brown partridge.
Antennae Horns: Pheasant-tail feather-fibres.

8 Amber Longhorn

COMMENT

This was Richard Walker's favourite imitation of the ascending sedge pupa. He would often use it when the sedge were thick on midsummer evenings at Grafham. I had some good catches during evening boat sessions at Pitsford in 1985. Conditions were near flat-calm and I retrieved the fly very slowly in an area of rising fish. It is an excellent pattern.

DRESSING

Hook: Size 14, 12 or 10.
Tying silk: Black.
Body: Amber ostrich herl ribbed with silver wire.
Thorax: Black ostrich herl.
Hackle: Brown partridge.
Antennae Horns: Pheasant-tail feather-fibres.

Sedge-time Specials

You cannot have too many change-flies at sedge time – it is part of the fun – and this is another important batch. The Cove Pheasant Tail is a fly you must try. You can fish it with complete confidence. The Soldier Palmer is a pattern everyone knows after its recent successes on the reservoirs. In the hands of anglers such as Brian Leadbetter and Bob Morey it is absolutely deadly. They catch trout so fast on it in high summer that it is almost unbelievable. For them this is the ultimate top dropper.

1   Olive Emerger

COMMENT

The new curved emerger hooks allow much better imitations of the nymph hatching into the adult winged fly than were previously possible. That pause of a second or two as the nymph lingers at the surface shedding its skin is when the trout sees the nymph as the easiest target.

DRESSING

Hook: Size 14, 12 or 10 curved emerger hook.
Tying silk: Black.
Body: Olive floss ribbed with a strand of green Flashabou.
Thorax: Olive seal's fur or substitute.
Hackle: Olive hen.
Wing: A pair of honey cock hackle-tips.
Head: Black varnish.

2   Soldier Palmer

COMMENT

The Soldier Palmer could well be Britain's most popular fly. Virtually every reservoir and loch fly-fisher ties the Soldier Palmer on to his top dropper at some time during the day from May onwards. Fished loch-style, this fly catches so many trout at the hands of an expert that it seems the trout are almost queuing up to take it!

DRESSING

Hook: Size 14, 12 or 10.
Tying silk: Black.
Tail and Body: Red wool ribbed with gold or silver oval tinsel.
Body hackle: Medium-brown cock, palmered.
Head: Black varnish.

1 Olive Emerger   **2** Soldier Palmer   **3** Green Peckham   **4** Yellow Peckham
Cove Pheasant Tail   **6** Skating Sedge   **7** Cinnamon Sedge Emerger   **8** All-black Sedge

3 Green Peckham

COMMENT

This is a colour variation of the Heckham Peckham. The green shade is a winner during the sedge period of July, August and September. Use the pattern as a middle dropper or point-fly on reservoir or loch.

DRESSING

Hook: Size 14, 12 or 10.
Tying silk: Black.
Tail: Golden-pheasant tippets.
Body: Green floss ribbed with brown tying silk.
Hackle: Light brown cock.
Wing: White-tipped mallard.
Head: Black varnish.

4 Yellow Peckham

COMMENT

This variation of the Heckham Peckham is a good summer pattern. It works particularly well after the first sedges have hatched. Use it as a general pattern on the point of a three-fly cast for wet-fly loch fishing. Like the Heckham, this is a first-class sea trout fly.

DRESSING

Hook: Size 14, 12 or 10.
Tying silk: Black.
Tail: Golden-pheasant tippets.
Body: Yellow floss ribbed with brown tying silk.
Hackle: Black cock.
Wing: White-tipped mallard.
Head: Black varnish.

5 Cove Pheasant Tail

COMMENT

Arthur Cove is acknowledged as our top nymph fisherman – his dedication to the method is unshakeable. This particular simple pattern is good enough to measure up to any nymph-fishing situation, as Arthur proves time and time again on a variety of waters. You can have faith in this nymph throughout the season.

DRESSING

Hook: Size 14, 12, 10 or 8 medium-shank.
Tying silk: Black.
Body: Pheasant-tail feather-fibre ribbed with copper wire. Begin the tying round the hook-bend.
Thorax: Grey mole or seal's fur.
Shellback head: Pheasant-tail feather-fibres.
Head: Black varnish.

6 Skating Sedge

COMMENT

I found this one in a box of reject flies given to me by David Train. It is among my top six favourite flies for drift-fishing in competitions. It really is very good used on point, centre dropper or bob according to the wave height.

DRESSING

Hook: Size 14, 12 or 10.
Tying silk: Brown.
Tail: Brown hackle-fibres.
Body: Dull orange floss.
Body hackle: Ginger-brown cock, palmered.
Wing: Natural brown bucktail.
Head: Clear varnish.

7 Cinnamon Sedge Emerger

COMMENT

This is an excellent pattern for evening fishing, especially as dusk approaches. The trout respond to it at this time on many of the reservoirs and pits I fish, with the last two weeks of July being the very best period. Grease your cast up to six inches from the fly and fish slowly through the rises.

DRESSING

Hook: Size 14, 12 or 10 curved emerger hook.
Tying silk: Black.
Body: Brown floss ribbed with fine silver wire.
Thorax: Brown seal's fur or substitute.
Hackle: Brown hen.
Wings: A pair of cree cock hackle-tips.
Head: Black varnish.

8 All-black Sedge

COMMENT

If ever you go to Caithness or Sutherland, in Scotland's far north, to fish the hill-lochs in summer, you will come across a tiny all-black sedge. I saw this fly in huge numbers when I fished Loch Watten and Lord Thurso's hill-lochs. This is the best imitation of it that I have seen.

DRESSING

Hook: Size 14, 12 or 10.
Tying silk: Black.
Body: Black floss.
Body hackle: Black cock.
Wing: Black feather-fibre.
Front hackle: Black cock.
Antennae: Strands of black feather-fibres.
Head: Black varnish.

Nymphs

Introduction to Nymphs

Trout feed on nymphs more than on anything else. That is a bold statement, but a factual one. Yet it wasn't until the great G.E.M. Skues devised a few artificials and caused a furore among his fellow fly-fishers that anyone considered nymph fishing as a technique.

One tip given to me many years ago by master fly-fisher Dick Shrive was that the evening rise really begins at 11 a.m. When I questioned this, he explained that many nymphs leave their larval cases and stay deep-down on the bottom weed before eventually swimming to the surface during the evening. Hungry trout sort out the nymphs at all stages – when they are deep-down, while they are rising to the surface, and when they are about to emerge in the surface film. Fishing tactics must be adapted to cover all these circumstances.

Sometimes I lightly weight my nymphs with copper wire. This makes them fish deeper than standard dressings and they do well on the point. Copper wire is by far the best material for adding weight to small nymph hooks (sizes 14 or 12). It is more delicate than lead.

A floating line usually serves best for bank fishing, but a sink-tip is better for deeper water, especially off dam walls. The new floating-line butt extensions from Spain are good in such situations. Imagine two metres of tapered hollow-braid of mixed copper wire and nylon. The butt end is slipped on to your WF8 fly-line, Superglued and then whipped. At the finer tip end is a delicate loop on to which you tie your leader. I found these extensions ideal for nymph fishing when I tried them during 1985. They give perfect presentation and control when fished in a side-wind.

Among my favourite general nymph patterns are the Black Buzzer, Pheasant Tail, Hare's Ear, Spring Favourite, Ivens' Green and Brown, Tiger Nymph and Sedge Pupa.

Other nymphs which have become popular on many small trout fisheries are the long-shanked, leaded varieties. These are tied on long-shanked size 8 hooks and weighted quite heavily with lead-foil strips cut from wine-bottle tops. These nymphs are fished singly on a floating fly-line, but they are difficult to cast, so you need a powerful rod and at least WF8 line. The idea is that you stalk a good-sized rainbow in the clear waters of fisheries such as those in Hampshire, Wiltshire and Gloucestershire and then cast in front of it as it cruises round, often deep-down in perhaps six or ten feet of water. Obviously you need a nymph that sinks very quickly.

The excitement of this type of fishing lies in the fact that you can see it all happen, as the trout takes or rejects your nymph. The long-shank patterns which I favour are the Westward Bug, Stickfly, Wonderbug, Green Beast, Damselfly Nymph, Shrimp, Walker's Mayfly Nymph and Black Leech.

In tying a nymph it is well to remember that the naturals are sombrely coloured and you therefore need similarly sombre material. Having said that, it has to be admitted that some of the naturals also have splashes of brighter colour. One of these is represented by my own Spring Favourite, which is the pattern I have chosen to describe here. The natural, which is a small green midge pupa, has a bright yellow patch on its thorax. This is represented on the artificial by a yellow false hackle.

I suggest that you start with a size 12 hook. Fix it in the vice and run a length of black tying silk on to the shank in tight, touching turns down to the bend. Now catch in a bunch of white cock hackle-fibres to form the tail followed by three inches of fine gold wire for the ribbing. The tail, incidentally, should be about the same length as the gape of the hook.

Now let the silk bobbin hang while you

prepare the body material. This consists of olive marabou dubbed on to the silk in the same way that you would dub seal's fur. The very fluffy fibres from the base of the feather are the best to use. Tear these off carefully, place them along the silk and twist the two together. Keep twisting them in the same direction, but at the same time allow the fibres to build up slightly in the centre of the length of the silk so that they taper towards the ends of the 'rope' which you have formed.

Now wind the dubbed 'rope' on to the hook-shank, starting at the tail and working towards the eye, building up slightly as you go to make a carrot shape, but stopping at about one-third of the length of the hook-shank from the eye. Complete the abdomen by winding on the fine gold wire ribbing in a spiral opposite to that in which the dubbed marabou was wound.

The top of the thorax and the developing wings of the nymph are represented by a slip of grey mallard primary feather. Take a ½-inch slip of feather, fold it in half, then in half again, and then catch-in the pointed end (just where the body material finishes) with a couple of turns of silk, so that the feather lies back over the shank. Now form the thorax itself from dubbed marabou as used for the body, but instead of making it

into a 'rope', form it into a small ball. Wind this on and then pull the slip of grey mallard feather tightly over the back and tie it down at the eye. Clip off the waste and invert the hook in the vice ready for the false hackle to be tied in. Form the false hackle from a small bunch of fibres torn from a cock hackle dyed yellow. Keep the points even and clip the butt ends of the fibres to the required length – so that the hackle-points just cover the hook-point when the fibres are tied in. Having done that, turn the fly right way up in the vice, build up a neat, tapered head, whip-finish and apply a couple of coats of Vycoat. Finally, when the head is dry, tease out a few marabou fibres from the body to roughen the appearance slightly.

If you want a leaded nymph, then the basic difference is that you bind slender strips of lead-foil on to the shank over the initial winding of tying silk. But you will find this technique described in detail, along with other tying methods, in *Imitations of a Trout's World*, written by Peter Gathercole and myself. Of course, if you want only a lightly-weighted nymph, then you can use copper wire as I have already mentioned. Happy nymphing! You should find enough patterns in the following selections to keep you busy!

Chironomid Nymphs

Chironomids in the various stages of their life-cycle form the trout's main food source throughout the year on many waters. This selection covers all those stages, from the bottom-dwelling bloodworm to the hatching midge, and all can be used with confidence throughout the season. A good choice for an early-season nymphing cast (for, say, late April) would be the Bloodworm on the point, the Footballer in the centre, and the Claret Hatching Midge on the top – and remember, fish them very slowly.

1 Mole Nymph

COMMENT

That old Ravensthorpe regular, Bert Clayson, gave me some very good advice when I started trout fishing: 'Always keep your nymphs sparsely dressed.' I often recall his words as, time after time, he is proved right. The Mole Nymph is one of these simple, sparse patterns. It catches plenty of trout and is especially good in a buzzer rise. It also works well when fish are well up in the surface area.

DRESSING

Hook: Size 14, 12 or 10 medium-shank bronze.
Tying silk: Black.
Body: Dubbed mole fur, built up into a carrot-shape and thickening towards the head.
Thorax: One turn of dark grey ostrich herl.
Head: Black varnish.

2 Hatching Orange Pupa

COMMENT

This nymph shows the correct shape of a chironomid about to hatch, so my advice is to fish it high in the water as the water begins to warm up during early May. Orange is not as unusual a colour for a nymph as you might think. Most pupae momentarily display a bright colour during that split-second before they hatch.

DRESSING

Hook: Size 14, 12 or 10.
Tying silk: Black.
Body: Orange floss, ribbed with silver wire.
Thorax shellback: Brown feather-fibre.
Wing-cases: White feather-fibre.
Breather Filament: White nylon wool.
Head: Black varnish.

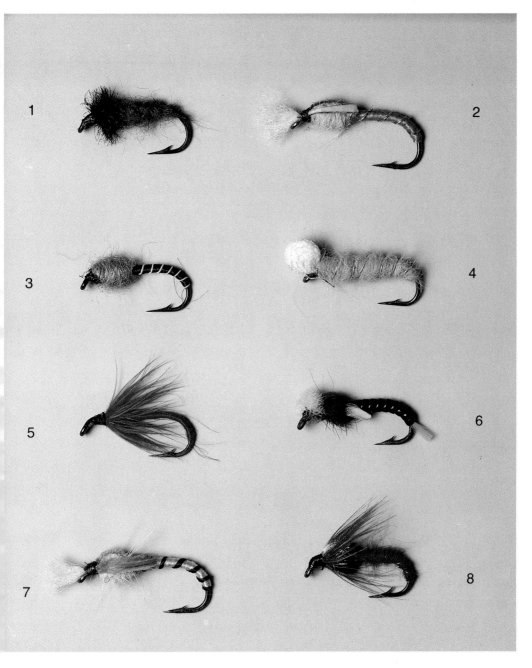

1 Mole Nymph **2** Hatching Orange Pupa **3** Footballer **4** Green Suspender Nymph
5 Bloodworm **6** Carnill's Buzzer **7** Hatching Green Pupa **8** Claret Hatching Midge

3 Footballer

COMMENT

Geoffrey Bucknall devised this pattern, and it is as good an imitator of the early-season small black chironomid as any I know. Geoff used both black and white horsehair for the body, but you can make do with black floss if you find hair difficult to get. Geoff had good results fishing the Footballer close to the surface, casting it just in front of a cruising fish. The leader should be greased to within six inches of the nymph when this style is adopted.

DRESSING

Hook: Size 14, 12 or 10.
Tying silk: Black.
Body: Black floss, ribbed with a strand of white horse hair (tail) or substitute.
Thorax: Grey mole fur.
Head: Black varnish.

4 Green Suspender Nymph

COMMENT

The Suspender Buzzer is a John Goddard classic. It can be tied in whatever colour you desire to make a complete range. A friend of mine, Nick Nicholson, fishes a team of these nymphs almost exclusively at Pitsford. This annoys his boat partners, but he does have some very good catches. I like to use the Suspender when fish are taking nymphs high in the water. Allow the breeze to fish the nymphs for you. The takes are confident and the trout hook themselves.

DRESSING

Hook: Size 14, 12 or 10.
Tying silk: Black.
Thorax and body: Green seal's fur, Antron or wool, ribbed with fine silver wire.
Head: A ball of polystyrene trapped in a piece of white nylon stocking.
Head finish: Black varnish.

5 Bloodworm

COMMENT

The Bloodworm is used mostly from the bank as a point-fly, but it also works in shallow bays from an anchored boat. Slow-and-deep is the method, so that the nymph 'crawls' along the bottom. I have caught trout with their stomachs crammed full of bloodworms, usually in the summer months.

DRESSING

Hook: Size 14, 12 or 10, weighted with copper wire.
Tying silk: Black or red.
Body: Red floss silk.
Hackle: Bright red cock.
Head: Black varnish.

6 Carnill's Buzzer

COMMENT

Bob Carnill, from Nottingham, is one of the country's leading fly-dressers. He has a one-track mind when he sees a new material: what sort of fly will it make? So when I sent him some Black Streak flat shooting-head nylon, it wasn't long before he sent me a set of Black Buzzers which were the most realistic representations of hatching flies I have seen. They work well when fished in the surface film to nymphing trout.

DRESSING

Hook: Size 14, 12 or 10, medium-shank bronze.
Tying silk: Black.
Tail: White nylon filaments.
Body: Black Streak flat nylon, wound tight.
Wing-cases: Two small sections of white Raffene.
Breathers: White nylon wool.
Head: Black varnish.

7 Hatching Green Pupa

COMMENT

When you are fishing a reservoir in hot and sunny, flat-calm conditions, with nothing doing on top and precious little deep-down, keep an eye open for bright-green and sometimes quite small chironomids. The hatch is never a big one, since this species is rarer than others, but when it does occur, fish this pattern slowly through the surface singly and on a size 14 hook and a 3lb leader.

DRESSING

Hook: Size 14, 12 or 10.
Tying silk: Black.
Body: Bright green floss, ribbed with black tying silk.
Thorax: Grey seal's fur or wool.
Shellback head: Brown feather-fibre.
Wing-cases: Orange feather-fibre.
Breather filament: White nylon wool.
Head: Black varnish.

8 Claret Hatching Midge

COMMENT

At Grafham in the late 1960s we used to enjoy some good late-evening rises to buzzer. At that time I found claret a killing colour, so I developed this hatching pattern and, in so doing, broke away from more accepted tyings. To give my nymph more movement on the slow retrieve, I use a full, circular hackle. This makes for a better imitation of the natural insect's wings emerging from their protective cases. Fish the nymph right in the surface film.

DRESSING

Hook: Size 14, 12 or 10, medium-shank bronze.
Tying silk: Black.
Body: Single strand of claret wool, ribbed with fuse-wire.
Thorax: Peacock herl with grey feather-fibre at the body side of the hackle. Pull this into the shellback head after the hackle has been wound on.
Hackle: Two turns of honey cock hackle.
Head: Bring forward the shellback feather, tie off and varnish black.

Deadly Nymphs

This is a fine batch of deceiver nymphs which would keep me happy throughout the season for bank fishing. All of them seem to work at any fishery. The Hare's Ear is the most versatile small nymph; I know some anglers who always include it on a nymph cast. My own Spring Favourite excels when clear water and bright overhead conditions are making things difficult. It has helped me out on numerous occasions. And then there is Tom Ivens' old pattern, the Green and Brown Nymph, which has really come back into favour. I did very well with it in 1985.

1 Eyebrook Nymph

COMMENT

The Eyebrook Nymph, born at the reservoir of its name, has some Jersey Herd lure characteristics. Why it should work so well, I am not sure. It is particularly killing when cast across the path of a fish moving upwind. The method is to drop the fly about a metre upwind of the moving fish and then strip in quite fast to induce a take.

DRESSING

Hook: Size 14, 12 or 10.
Tying silk: Black.
Tail and back: Bronze peacock herl.
Body: Amber seal's fur ribbed with No 2 gold tinsel.
Head: Bronze peacock herl.

2 Spring Favourite

COMMENT

Trout are not always easy to tempt when they are on tiny black buzzers, yet if numbers of green buzzers are hatching during spring or summer, catching fish is as easy as shelling peas. When fish can be seen rising and taking the green buzzer just beneath the surface, fish my Spring Favourite on a floating line and drop it a couple of feet upwind of the rise-form. A confident take is a near-certainty. This nymph has been quite devastating under these conditions at both Rutland and Pitsford.

DRESSING

Hook: Size 14, 12 or 10, medium-shank bronze.
Tying silk: Black.
Tail: A few fibres of white cock hackle.
Body: Single strand of dark olive wool ribbed with fine gold wire.
Thorax: Build up with olive body wool and top with a light grey feather-fibre for the shellback wing-cases.
Hackle: Short-fibred pale yellow hen hackle-fibres. Throat only.
Head: Black varnish.

1 Eyebrook Nymph   2 Spring Favourite   3 Damselfly Nymph   4 The Poacher
5 Hare's Ear Nymph   6 Copper-wire Nymph   7 Olive Nymph
8 Iven's Green and Brown Nymph

3 Damselfly Nymph

COMMENT

Nick Nicholson introduced me to this nymph in the mid-1970s. Today a number of long-shank, leaded versions are available, but it is still worth tying-up a few of this pattern as well. The time to use it is when the natural damsel nymph is seen swimming along the surface, usually in July or August.

DRESSING

Hook: Size 12 or 10, short-shank.
Tying silk: Black.
Tail: Olive cock hackle-fibres.
Body: Olive floss or wool.
Body Hackle: Olive cock palmered and trimmed.
Head: Black varnish.

4 The Poacher

COMMENT

It is ironic that Frank Cutler should have given me this pattern to try, as he is such a good and experienced game-fisher that his closest friends are allowed to refer to him as the 'Old Poacher'. Frank 'discovered' this fly on Orkney's Loch of Harray when he was fishing there with the English team. The fly apparently has a high reputation in Scotland.

DRESSING

Hook: Size 14, 12 or 10.
Tying silk: Black.
Tail: Red feather-fibre.
Body: Amber floss tied carrot-shape.
Thorax: Peacock herl.
Hackle: Furnace hen.
Head: Black varnish.

5 Hare's Ear Nymph

COMMENT

This is the drab nymph that many expert fly-fishers rave about. They just wouldn't be without it for bank fishing at the big reservoirs. John Wadham and John Wilshaw have taken some exceptionally good catches from Rutland Water these past few years simply by patiently fishing this nymph. All you need is a floating fly-line, a long leader, a very slow retrieve, and lots of confidence.

DRESSING

Hook: Size 14, 12 or 10.
Tying silk: Black.
Tail: Ginger cock hackle-fibres or squirrel-tail hair.
Body: Fur from hare's ear or face, made carrot-shape.
Thorax: Fur from hare's ear or face.
Wing-cases: Grey feather-fibre.
Head: Black varnish.

6 Copper-wire Nymph

COMMENT

This nymph was used by Oliver Kite, the well-known chalk-stream fly-fisher. It has little dressing, but it does sink quickly, so he developed a technique known as the induced-take. The method is to retrieve in figure-of-eight style, every so often lifting the rod-tip a foot or so. Any following trout that is really interested will take on the lift.

DRESSING

Hook: Size 14, 12 or 10.
Tying silk: Black.
Tail: Pheasant-tail feather-fibres.
Body: Copper wire ribbed with silver wire.
Thorax: Copper wire.
Head: Black varnish.

7 Olive Nymph

COMMENT

This nymph has many uses, but it is important to give it a try in late May when the pond olives start hatching, especially when you are bank-fishing. Later in the summer it can be good during good hatches of large olive chironomids such as we had in 1985 on Grafham and Pitsford. It is a good all-round nymph in which I have every confidence.

DRESSING

Hook: Size 14, 12 or 10.
Tying silk: Black.
Tail: Olive hackle-fibres.
Body: Olive wool, seal's fur or substitute.
Hackle: Olive hen.
Head: Black varnish.

8 Iven's Green and Brown Nymph

COMMENT

This nymph is simple to tie, yet it has a most impressive record of catching trout on all waters. It imitates the larvae of caddis if fished deep, or a hatching nymph if fished close to the surface. Because of its shape, it will even pass as a fish fry.

DRESSING

Hook: Size 10, medium-shank bronze.
Tying silk: Black.
Tail and back: Tie in a bunch of bronze peacock herl. Trim tail to required length and leave the back hanging loose.
Body: Green and brown ostrich herl, ribbed with fine fuse-wire. The final operation is to pull the peacock back tight, secure it at the head, trim and tie off.
Head: Black varnish.

Deceiver Nymphs

This is a selection of general patterns from which a cast of three flies can easily be made up for sedge-time in July and onwards. Try a Crawling Caddis on the point, Goddard's Orange Sedge in the centre, and Dr Bell's Amber Nymph on the top. The latter is still one of the best stillwater sedge pupa imitations, and we shall all be eternally grateful to Dr Bell for his contribution to early nymph patterns. The Copydex Nymph may be thought rather weird and wonderful by some. To tie it is to enter into the realms of model-making.

1   Crawling Caddis

COMMENT

The Crawling Caddis, as its name suggests, is a nymph to be fished hard along the bottom. In shallow water a floating line and long leader can be used with the pattern on the point. If you are not sure of the depth, use a medium-sink line from the bank or a fast-sinker from an anchored boat. The caddis grub is a very slow-moving creature – retrieve accordingly!

DRESSING

Hook: Size 12 or 10 long-shank, weighted with copper wire.
Tying silk: Black.
Tail: Brown marabou.
Body: Bronze peacock herl ribbed with silver wire.
Thorax: Yellow seal's fur or wool.
Hackle: Brown partridge.
Head: Black varnish.

2   Red Spider

COMMENT

My old friend, Frank Cutler, took five fish at Grafham on a Red Spider a few years ago in a flat calm. Conditions had looked hopeless until he began to fish the pattern (size 14) dry and static. His catch qualified him for a place in the English International team. The alternative hackles give you a choice of method, both of which work well. Tie some flies in each style.

DRESSING

Hook: Size 14, 12 or 10.
Tying silk: Black.
Tail: Bright red cock hackle-fibres.
Body: Red floss ribbed with fine silver wire.
Hackle: Light brown cock (for a fly to be fished dry or close to the surface) or hen (for a fly to be fished deeper, rather as a nymph).
Head: Black varnish.

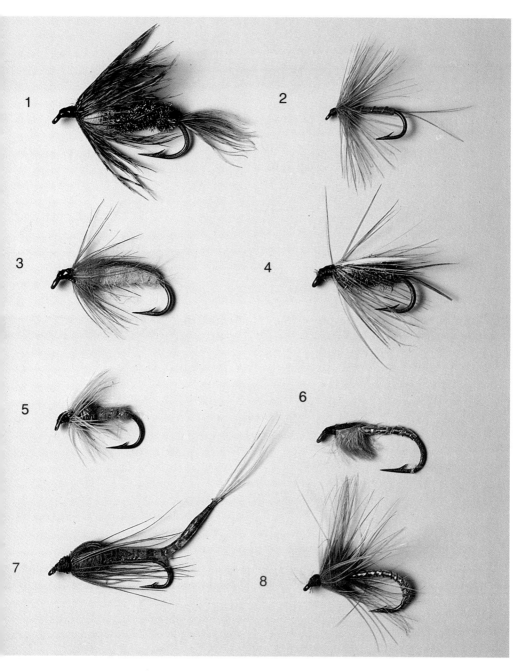

1 Crawling Caddis   2 Red Spider   3 Amber Nymph   4 Prince Nymph
5 Goddard's Orange Sedge   6 Silver Nymph   7 Copydex Nymph   8 Half Palmer

3 Amber Nymph

COMMENT

Dr Bell, of Blagdon, was one of the early thinkers of stillwater trout fishing, devising both sedge and chironomid pupa patterns. He loved his fishing so much that occasionally he was late visiting his patients. This was his sedge pupa. He used the amber and brown body. The pattern has stood the test of time from the mid-1920s to date. Do try the variant with the orange thorax.

DRESSING

Hook: Size 14, 12 or 10.
Tying silk: Black.
Body: Amber seal's fur.
Thorax: Brown or rusty-orange seal's fur.
Shellback: Brown feather-fibre.
Hackle: Honey hen.
Head: Black varnish.

4 Prince Nymph

COMMENT

This American nymph is so popular on the other side of the Atlantic that many British fly-fishers have become inquisitive about it and have begun to try it. It can be tied in differing colours and the goose biots give a very good effect. It is a good fly to use during a buzzer rise.

DRESSING

Hook: Size 14, 12 or 10.
Tying silk: Black.
Tail: Olive goose biots.
Body: Bronze peacock herl.
Wing-cases: Two white goose biots.
Hackle: Olive cock.
Head: Black varnish.

5 Goddard's Orange Sedge

COMMENT

The first time I tried this John Goddard pattern was at Two Lakes in Hampshire, when a good-sized trout was rising occasionally well out in the lake. I was fishing the nymph by itself, so I put out a good cast and made sure my long leader turned over well. The nymph must have landed close to the fish's nose, for the fly disappeared in a great swirl of water and I was into a 4lb rainbow. That lucky start gave me confidence in this pattern, and it has rarely let me down.

DRESSING

Hook: Size 14, 12 or 10.
Tying silk: Black.
Body: Orange seal's fur ribbed with silver oval tinsel.
Thorax: Pheasant-tail feather-fibre.
Hackle: Blue-dun hen.
Head: Black varnish.

6 Silver Nymph

COMMENT

An unusual nymph this, and one that doesn't look much like any natural insect, but it works well at daphnia time in mid and late summer and it is well worth having it in your box. Perhaps the pink blob of thorax is taken to be just another speck of daphnia.

DRESSING

Hook: Size 14, 12 or 10.
Tying silk: Black.
Body: Silver Lurex ribbed with pink floss.
Thorax: Pink ostrich herl.
Shellback: Brown feather-fibre.
Head: Black varnish.

7 Copydex Nymph

COMMENT

Clear Copydex has many uses in the tying – or rather modelling – of realistic-looking flies and nymphs, and when the end-product looks as convincing to our eyes as this pattern does, it just has to be good for deceiving trout. I believe this material will be used more in the years to come.

DRESSING

Hook: Size 12, long-shank.
Tying silk: Black or olive.
Tail and body: Olive cock hackles marked with a felt pen and covered with clear Copydex.
Hackle: Olive cock.
Head: Black or clear varnish.

8 Half Palmer

COMMENT

Bev Perkins tied up a series of flies based on this dressing in 1982 and gave me a few to try. A green version was good at sedge-time, but I found this red one the best all-rounder. At times I substituted it for the Soldier Palmer and achieved similar results. This half-palmer style is a good idea.

DRESSING

Hook: Size 12 or 10.
Tying silk: Black.
Body: Gold Lurex ribbed with black tying silk.
Thorax: Bright red seal's fur.
Hackle: Furnace.
Head: Black varnish.

Buzzers

Buzzers or chironomid nymphs – call them what you will – are the trout's most common food in most English reservoirs. Colours vary according to the hatch. Dressings are tending to become more 'fancy', but the simple traditional pattern is as good as any and an easy pattern to tie if you are only just beginning as a fly-tyer. One tip: make sure that you use hooks of sizes 14, 12 and 10. A size 14 Buzzer will sometimes catch you eight trout when a 10 will leave you blank.

1 Grey Buzzer

COMMENT

Grey-coloured buzzers are common on many waters, and at Ravensthorpe in particular. Some anglers feel colour is not important, but I do not agree. As time has passed, I have become ever more convinced that the right colour fly, nymph or lure makes all the difference between an excellent catch and a moderate one.

DRESSING

Hook: Size 14, 12 or 10.
Tying silk: Black.
Tail filaments: White feather-fibre.
Body: Grey floss ribbed with silver wire.
Thorax: Bronze peacock herl.
Head filaments: White feather-fibre.
Head: Black varnish.

2 Claret Buzzer

COMMENT

This buzzer fishes well in the surface film. Fish it singly and silicone-grease your leader to within six inches of the nymph. Trout rising to buzzers hit them just before the nymph reaches the surface. The surface film is a barrier to ascending nymphs, and they often struggle there for several seconds, becoming easy prey for the trout. Once trout are used to taking just below the surface, this is where you must present your artificial. When you see the 'boil' type of rise, you can be sure it's time to try this method.

DRESSING

Hook: Size 14, 12 or 10.
Tying silk: Black.
Tail filaments: White feather-fibre.
Body: Claret floss or wool ribbed with silver wire.
Thorax: Bronze peacock herl.
Head filaments: White feather-fibre.
Head: Black varnish.

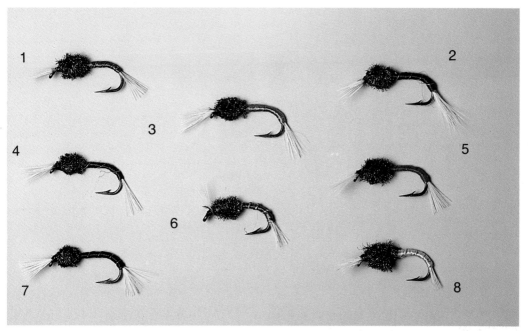

1 Grey   **2** Claret   **3** Green   **4** Brown
5 Red   **6** Olive   **7** Black Buzzer Nymph   **8** Ghost White

3 Green Buzzer

COMMENT

After the mass hatches of the early-season black buzzers, which last nearly to the end of April, we begin to see a few greenish buzzers on many of our large stillwaters. David Reinger told me of some good catches of bigger-than-average trout he had at Pitsford on the Green Buzzer. He was using a sink-tip line in the deep water out from Gorse Bank in early May and the trout would take only the Green Buzzer, no matter what other flies he tried.

DRESSING

Hook: Size 14, 12 or 10.
Tying silk: Black.
Tail filaments: White feather-fibre.
Body: Green floss or wool ribbed with silver tinsel.
Thorax: Bronze peacock herl.
Head: Black varnish.

4 Brown Buzzer

COMMENT

The Brown Buzzer is one of three nymphs I have mentioned as a favourite team, so here is the most successful method to use to fish it. Select an area of the reservoir with a good left-to-right crosswind. Find a headland, and cast square to the wind with a floating line. Allow the line to drift your nymphs round naturally, at the same speed as the waves. Trout cruising upwind will see such an offering as natural food, and will take confidently. You will achieve a better-than-average hooking ratio if you allow the line to develop a curve.

DRESSING

Hook: Size 14, 12 or 10.
Tying silk: Black.
Tail filaments: White feather-fibre.
Body: Brown floss ribbed with silver wire.
Thorax: Bronze peacock herl.
Head filaments: White feather-fibre.
Head: Black varnish.

5 Red Buzzer

COMMENT

This was Cyril Inwood's favourite buzzer, and he had some terrific catches with it. I shall never forget one particular day at Eyebrook Reservoir, when a group of us were fishing with Cyril from the bank on the wood side. Cyril had forty fish while the rest of us struggled to take between three and five apiece. Cyril craftily told us he was using a Claret Nymph, but he really had on a bright red pattern which he was fishing slow-and-deep. Many of his fish were full of bloodworms.

DRESSING

Hook: Size 14, 12 or 10.
Tying silk: Black.
Tail filaments: White feather-fibre.
Body: Red floss or wool ribbed with silver tinsel.
Thorax: Bronze peacock herl.
Head filaments: White feather-fibre.
Head: Black varnish.

6   Olive Buzzer

A killing buzzer nymph set-up which
experienced reservoir fly-fishers use in late April
is black on the point, olive in the centre, and
brown on the top. It is certainly a good team with
which to begin. Many is the time it has given me
enough success during an evening bank-fishing
session to make any change of fly unnecessary.

DRESSING

Hook: Size 14, 12 or 10.
Tying silk: Black.
Tail filament: White feather-fibre.
Body: Olive floss ribbed with silver wire.
Thorax: Bronze peacock herl.
Head filament: White feather-fibre.
Head: Black varnish.

7   Black Buzzer Nymph

COMMENT

This is the most common colour of early-season
hatches of this aquatic insect. Most regular bank
anglers include a Black Buzzer on their casts if
they are using three flies. The pattern is best
fished on a floating line, and it pays to change its
position on the cast to allow it to fish at different
depths.

DRESSING

Hook: Size 14, 12 or 10, medium-shank
bronze.
Tail: None, or few whisks of white fibre.
Body: Black silk or strand of wool ribbed with
silver fuse-wire.
Thorax: Bronze peacock herl topped with
small section of white wool or feather.
Head: Black varnish.

8   Ghost White Buzzer

COMMENT

White has proved such a killing colour with trout
that I experimented with it on my buzzer
nymphs. To my surprise, a pure-white buzzer,
fished in the same way as the more usual black,
brown or green varieties, worked just as well,
and perhaps better on occasion.

DRESSING

Hook: Size 10, 12 or 14, medium-shank
bronze.
Tying silk: Black.
Tail (optional): Spray of fine white hackle-
fibres.
Body: One strand of pure-white nylon wool
(as for the Baby Doll), wound round hook-
bend and ribbed with fuse-wire.
Thorax: Bronze peacock herl
Wing-cases: Spray of fine white hackle-
fibres, or a small piece of teased white wool.
Head: Black varnish.

Favourite Nymphs

This collection includes representations of several different types of aquatic insect, with two versions of the tantalising anglers' curse, the Caenis. The Stonefly Creeper is best used on the northern rivers, but I particularly like the Tiger Nymph because it imitates an ascending buzzer so well. I used it when I won my first major competition, the Gladding Masters' Event at Draycote in the early 1970s. John Goddard's PVC Nymph is excellent during the main daytime period and when olive buzzers are coming off as they so often do on Grafham in June.

1   Fluorescent Green Nymph

COMMENT

One of my lesser-known patterns, this one dates back to the mid-1970s. I don't use it as much nowadays, but when I recall the fish I used to catch on it, I think that perhaps I am wrong not to try it more often.

DRESSING

Hook: Size 14, 12 or 10.
Tying silk: Black.
Body: Silver Lurex ribbed with silver wire.
Thorax: Fluorescent green chenille.
Hackle: Blue-dun hen.
Head: Black varnish.

2   Stonefly Creeper

COMMENT

This very good stonefly pattern works well on northern and Scottish rivers. The stoneflies abound in rough streams, where their larvae can be found under the stones. They crawl ashore to transform into adults, hence the nickname 'Creeper'.

DRESSING

Hook: Size 14, 12 or 10.
Tying silk: Black.
Tail: Two fine brown hackle-feather stalks.
Body: Stripped quill of bronze peacock herl.
Thorax: Bronze peacock herl.
Hackle: Brown partridge.
Head: Black varnish.

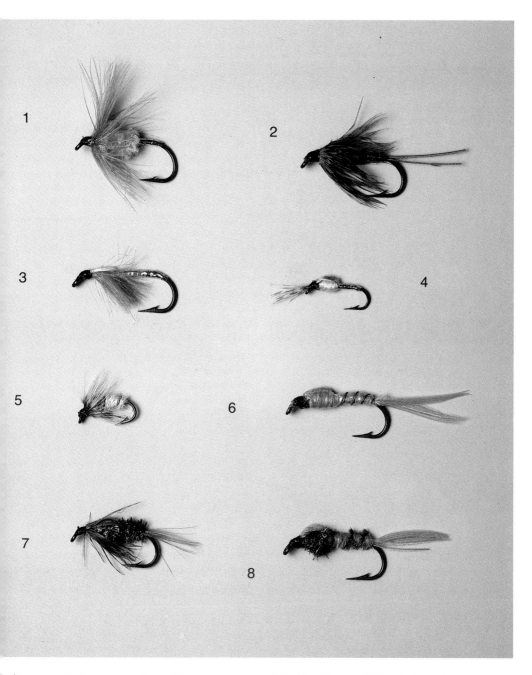

1 Fluorescent Green Nymph   2 Stonefly Creeper   3 Golden Pupa   4 Caenis Nymph
5 Hatching Caenis   6 Olive PVC Nymph   7 Tiger Nymph   8 Sepia Nymph

3 Golden Pupa

COMMENT

This David Train pattern is one of the few nymphs that I strip back fast. It works best in warm weather, so June onwards is the time to try it. Fish tend to follow and reject it when it is fished slowly, but they really crash into it when it is moving fast.

DRESSING

Hook: Size 14, 12 or 10.
Tying silk: Black.
Body: Gold Lurex ribbed with gold wire.
Thorax: Orange ostrich herl.
Shellback: Grey feather-fibre.
Head: Black varnish.

4 Caenis Nymph

COMMENT

The dreaded Caenis fly (or 'anglers' curse', as it is nicknamed) is a tiny insect that hatches in millions on a summer evening. Trout rise everywhere to them, but often many fly-fishers flog away, covering fish after fish, all in vain. At such times, fine down your tackle to a 2½lb breaking-strain leader and a light floating line and try this tiny nymph fished slowly right in the surface film.

DRESSING

Hook: Size 18, 16 or 14, normal-shank bronze.
Tying silk: Black or white.
Tail: None.
Body: For two-thirds, fine silver Lurex. Now build up a tiny ball-shaped white floss thorax and tie in a fine spray of teal feather-fibres. Pull these over to form shellback head.
Head: Black or white.

5 Hatching Caenis

COMMENT

Fish this pattern right on the top during that maddening hour or so when the Caenis are hatching so thickly that you are covered in them. Cast out and leave the fly static. Any fish mopping up will eventually find it. Do not be tempted into trying to cover feeding fish. If you do, then almost certainly you will not catch. A fine leader is essential.

DRESSING

Hook: Size 16.
Tying silk: Black.
Body: White ostrich herl ribbed with silver wire.
Thorax: Bronze peacock herl.
Hackle: Badger hen.
Head: Black varnish.

5 Olive PVC Nymph

COMMENT

his is one of John Goddard's many original
atterns, and one of his best; and since it sinks
uickly, it should always be used as a point-fly.
is a marvellous pattern at clear gravel-pit trout
sheries which have good hatches of pond
lives, and it can be used with confidence from
May onwards.

DRESSING

Hook: Size 14, 12 or 10, weighted with
copper wire.
Tying silk: Black.
Tail: Olive condor herl, tapered.
Body and thorax: Olive condor herl ribbed
with copper wire.
Body covering: A fine strip of clear PVC
stretched tight and wound on.
Shellback over thorax: Pheasant-tail
feather-fibre.
Head: Black varnish.

7 Tiger Nymph

COMMENT

have used this pattern successfully for four
easons. It seems particularly attractive to larger
out, especially browns. I can recall occasions
hen both a lure and the ordinary buzzer nymph
ailed from the bank, but a Tiger Nymph, fished
lowly on a floating line and long leader, brought
esults. On one such occasion a size 14 on the
oint produced four browns of more than 3lb.
ry the Tiger Nymph until the end of summer. It
especially good when the buzzer is about.

DRESSING

Hook: Size 14, 12 or 10, medium-shank
bronze.
Tying silk: Black.
Tail: A few sparse white hackle-fibres.
Body: Bronze peacock herl.
Thorax: Built-up peacock herl with a grey
feather-fibre shellback wing-case.
Hackle: Sparse speckled partridge fibres.
Throat only.
Head: Black varnish.

8 Sepia Nymph

COMMENT

'any versions of the Sepia Nymph are tied. This
he was given to me at Damerham back in the
ays when Colin Harms was there. Present it on
elicate tackle and fish it slowly and patiently. It
eems to do best on southern waters.

DRESSING

Hook: Size 14, 12 or 10.
Tying silk: Black.
Tail: Buff-coloured condor herl, tapered.
Body: Buff-coloured condor feather-fibre
ribbed with bronze peacock herl.
Thorax: Bronze peacock herl.
Shellback: Buff condor herl feather-fibre.
Head: Black varnish.

Bugs and Grubs

Important stillwater 'bugs' such as the corixae are eaten by trout in large numbers at certain times of the year, and artificials begin to come into their own as trout-catchers in early summer. Corixae imitations are particularly good patterns to try, for the natural insects are widely distributed, and certainly all the new shallow gravel-pits are alive with them. Often it pays to tie up a few buoyant patterns and some with differing body colours. In this selection I have included the usual Corixa artificial and the White Chomper (which was Dick Walker's general version), as well as snail, beetle and grub imitations.

1 Black Latex Crawler

COMMENT

Early in the season, when the water is cold and few aquatic animals are stirring, overwintered fish, and even newly-introduced stockies, really struggle to find food. At these times a slow bottom-crawling pattern, black for preference, is better than anything I know. Fish the fly as you would a Black and Peacock Spider – slow and deep on a sink-tip or slow-sink shooting-head. The shooting-head in particular will enable you to make a long cast, giving a long retrieve and much bottom-searching.

DRESSING

Hook: Size 14, 12 or 10 medium-shank.
Tying silk: Black.
Body: Black latex.
Thorax: Black ostrich or peacock herl.
Hackle: One turn of speckled partridge.
Head: Black varnish.

2 Stonefly Nymph

COMMENT

This nymph was given to me by John Cook, of Derby. He is a perfectionist fly-dresser with many original ideas, and this pattern is incredibly realistic. The natural is found principally in fast-flowing northern and Scottish rivers, where it is sought after by the wild brown trout. Use the artificial on a floating or sink-tip line and fish the slacks rather than the main current.

DRESSING

Hook: Size 10 or 8 long-shank bronze.
Tying silk: Black.
Tail: Two sturdy bronze mallard feather-fibres.
Body: Brown latex; narrow, but carrot-shaped.
Thorax: Mole fur, dubbed on.
Legs: Mallard from back primary. Knot feathers as shown.
Head: Shellback; brown latex topped with clear varnish.

1 Black Latex Crawler   2 Stonefly Nymph   3 Grafham Snail   4 Coch-y-bondhu
5 The Corixa   6 White Chomper   7 Black Chomper   8 Olive Latex Grub

Nymphs

3 Grafham Snail

COMMENT

The time to try this fly is when snails float to the surface and then migrate by floating downwind across the big reservoirs. Use a floating fly-line, grease your leader, and even silicone spray the fly to keep it fishing just beneath the surface. I have used this pattern with success not only at Grafham, but also at Draycote and Blagdon.

DRESSING

Hook: Size 14, 12 or 10.
Tying silk: Black.
Body: Black chenille.
Shellback: Black feather-fibre.
Hackle: Black cock.
Head: Black varnish.

4 Coch-y-bondhu

COMMENT

One of the best-known traditional beetle bug patterns, much used in Wales and to a lesser extent in Scotland, the Coch-y-bondhu has a number of local names in Wales, where it is often first choice on the cast in June and July. The fly imitates a small terrestrial insect which appears in large numbers in June. The naturals are blown on to the surface of the peat-stained lakes and llyns, and in no time at all trout are rising for them. Although the pattern is primarily a surface fly, to be fished on a floating line, I have heard of some good catches falling to it on a sinking line.

DRESSING

Hook: Size 14, 12 or 10.
Tying silk: Black.
Tag: Gold Lurex.
Body: Bronze peacock herl.
Hackle: Coch-y-bondhu hen.
Head: Black varnish.

5 The Corixa

COMMENT

The natural, also known as the water boatman, is prolific on many stillwaters. The artificial can be used with success throughout the season. It is best fished on a floating line and retrieved with a long-pull action which lifts the fly from deep-down to close to the surface. At Lower Moor, near Cirencester, I have seen the shallows, alive, with corixae, but the trout never came in to feed on them until the light began to fade. Then, browns of 3lb-plus came from less than two feet of water.

DRESSING

Hook: Size 14, 12 or 10 medium-shank.
Tying silk: Black.
Tag: Silver tinsel.
Body: White wool wound to a carrot shape and ribbed with fine silver wire.
Back: Any brown feather-fibre; oak turkey is good.
Legs: Pheasant-tail fibres or goose biots.
Hackle: Honey or light ginger cock hackle-fibres. Beard only.
Head: Black varnish.

6 White Chomper

COMMENT

This member of the Chomper family is intended to imitate the active corixa beetle. Corixae are found in the shallow, weedy margins of many of our stillwaters. They are a common trout food, and when the fish are on them, the White Chomper is a good nymph to try.

DRESSING

Hook: Size 14, 12 or 10.
Tying silk: Black or white.
Body: White ostrich herl ribbed with silver wire.
Shellback: White feather-fibre or Raffene.
Head: Black or clear varnish.

7 Black Chomper

COMMENT

This is another snail pattern and one of the Chomper series introduced by Richard Walker. It should be fished on a floating line when snails are seen floating at or just below the surface. You may sometimes spoon a trout and find it full of snails, yet see none floating at the surface. At such times, use a sinking line and get your fly well down. Trout will feed on snails on the bottom as well.

DRESSING

Hook: Size 14, 12 or 10.
Tying silk: Black.
Body: Black ostrich herl ribbed with silver wire.
Shellback: Black feather-fibre or Raffene.
Head: Black varnish.

8 Olive Latex Grub

COMMENT

This life-like olive grub takes fish when the pond olives are beginning to hatch in late May. By accident, while fishing at Pitsford, I found it to be also a first-class sedge pupa imitation. Fish it on a floating or sink-tip line and retrieve it very slowly with a figure-of-eight action.

DRESSING

Hook: Size 12 or 10.
Tying silk: Black.
Body: Clear latex strip.
Thorax: Olive ostrich herl.
Hackle: Grey partridge.
Head: Black varnish.

Long-shanked Pheasant Tails

Tied on a wide range of hook sizes and with varying colours for the thorax, the Pheasant Tail can be used to represent various aquatic creatures over a full season. For instance, with a white thorax, the PT can be used as a 'pinhead' fry pattern; with olive or yellow, as a sedge pupa; with grey or black, as a bottom-crawling larva. The PT is a 'must'!

1 White Pheasant Tail

COMMENT

This particular Pheasant Tail has a wide variety of uses. Probably the most important is as an imitation of a newly-hatched 'pinhead' coarse-fish fry. The 'pinhead' shoals are about in the shallows during July, when the method is to fish a single nymph on a long leader.

DRESSING

Hook: Size 14, 12, 10 or 8 long-shank.
Tying silk: Black.
Tail: Pheasant-tail feather-fibres.
Body: Pheasant-tail feather-fibres ribbed with fine copper wire.
Thorax: White seal's fur or substitute.
Hackle: Medium-brown hen.
Head: Black varnish.

2 Claret Pheasant Tail

COMMENT

Claret has a fine record in both wet and dry flies, and I can promise you that it works well in this variation of the famous Pheasant Tail Nymph as well. Fish the Claret PT slowly on a floating line as a point-fly in the larger sizes or as a dropper in the smaller.

DRESSING

Hook: Size 14, 12, 10 or 8 long-shank.
Tying silk: Black.
Tail: Pheasant-tail feather-fibres.
Body: Pheasant-tail feather-fibres ribbed with fine copper wire.
Thorax: Claret seal's fur or substitute.
Hackle: Medium-brown hen.
Head: Black varnish.

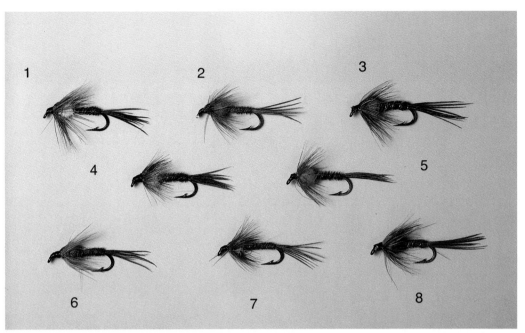

1 White **2** Claret **3** Grey **4** Yellow
5 Orange **6** Natural **7** Olive **8** Black

3 Grey Pheasant Tail

COMMENT

The colour combination of the Grey PT was first publicised by Arthur Cove. To say it works well would be an understatement. The pattern here differs from the Cove Nymph in that it is tied on a long-shank hook and has a hackle. It is good as a sedge larva imitation, but in smaller sizes it serves excellently as an ascending chironomid nymph.

DRESSING

Hook: Size 14, 12, 10 or 8 long-shank.
Tying silk: Black.
Tail: Pheasant-tail feather-fibres.
Body: Pheasant-tail feather-fibres ribbed with fine copper wire.
Thorax: Grey rabbit fur.
Hackle: Medium-brown hen.
Head: Black varnish.

4 Yellow Pheasant Tail

COMMENT

The Yellow Pheasant Tail is at its best during sedge time – mid-July to September. My successes with it have come in the evenings to a size 12 or 10. Sedge hatches often occur during a flat calm. This is the time to fish the nymph just beneath the surface with a figure-of-eight retrieve.

DRESSING

Hook: Size 14, 12, 10 or 8 long-shank.
Tying silk: Black.
Tail: Pheasant-tail feather-fibres.
Body: Pheasant-tail feather-fibres ribbed with fine copper wire.
Thorax: Yellow seal's fur or substitute.
Hackle: Honey hen hackle.
Head: Black varnish.

5 Orange Pheasant Tail

COMMENT

This is a multi-purpose nymph and should be used as such for best results. My friends and I have taken some fine catches of rainbows from Grafham in midsummer by stripping a size 8 in lure fashion through the upper levels in water which was 20 feet deep. The orange blob certainly attracts daphnia-feeding rainbows.

DRESSING

Hook: Size 14, 12, 10 or 8 long-shank.
Tying silk: Black.
Tail: Pheasant-tail feather-fibres.
Body: Pheasant-tail feather-fibres ribbed with fine copper wire.
Thorax: Orange seal's fur or substitute.
Hackle: Medium-brown hen.
Head: Black varnish.

6 Natural Pheasant Tail

COMMENT

The Pheasant Tail has been used by top fly-fishers for many years. While Frank Sawyer mastered the southern chalk-streams with it, Arthur Cove was mastering the Midlands reservoirs. The Pheasant Tail is simply a very good nymph imitation which passes as a larva when fished deep. It is easy to tie and is probably the most commonly used nymph. It can be weighted with copper wire to make it sink deep more quickly. I have the greatest faith in it.

DRESSING

Hook: Size 14, 12, 10, 8 long-shank.
Tying silk: Black.
Tail: Pheasant-tail feather-fibres.
Body: Pheasant-tail feather-fibres ribbed with fine copper wire.
Thorax: Pheasant-tail feather-fibres.
Hackle: Medium-brown hen.
Head: Black varnish.

7 Olive Pheasant Tail

COMMENT

In the late 1960s, I held the theory that because the entire underwater world was filled with shades of green, flies with green in their dressings would blend into the background and perhaps not be seen by the trout. I was completely wrong, and since then some of my most successful imitative patterns have included green. This is one of them. You can use it with confidence throughout the season.

DRESSING

Hook: Size 14, 12, 10 or 8 long-shank.
Tying silk: Black.
Tail: Pheasant-tail feather-fibres.
Body: Pheasant-tail feather-fibres ribbed with fine copper wire.
Thorax: Olive seal's fur or substitute.
Hackle: Honey hen.
Head: Black varnish.

8 Black Pheasant Tail

COMMENT

I like to fish this pattern slow and deep in its larger sizes (10 and 8), when it imitates a slow-moving, bottom-dwelling creepy-crawly. In smaller sizes (14 and 12) it serves as an ascending chironomid nymph or, if fished right on top, a hatching chironomid (buzzer).

DRESSING

Hook: Size 14, 12, 10 or 8 long-shank.
Tying silk: Black.
Tail: Pheasant-tail feather-fibres.
Body: Pheasant-tail feather-fibres ribbed with fine copper wire.
Thorax: Black seal's fur or substitute.
Hackle: Medium-brown or black hen.
Head: Black varnish.

Long-shanked Leaded Nymphs

These fast-sinking nymphs with leaded bodies are the ideal means of getting down quickly to cruising trout. Such fish are virtually always close to the bank, but right on the bottom, and if you use ordinary, non-weighted nymphs, your target fish will be out of vision before you have a chance to cover it. So, if you visit one of the small clear-water fisheries and want to do really well, don't be without a selection of these proven patterns. It was the Westward Bug which gave me my heaviest rainbow at 16¾lb.

1 Superla Bug

COMMENT

My best catch on this nymph was 16 rainbows between 2lb and 4½lb from Bayham Lake. I have also taken rainbows into double figures on it at Avington. I have found it excellent in varying conditions, fishing it singly on a long leader and with a very slow retrieve.

DRESSING

Hook: Size 10 or 8 long-shank with lightly leaded underbody.
Tying silk: Black.
Tail: Fluorescent orange hackle-fibres.
Body: Brown Superla dubbing built up into a carrot shape and ribbed with gold oval tinsel.
Hackle: Three turns of hot-orange cock.
Head: Black varnish.

2 Partridge and Orange

COMMENT

The original Partridge and Orange was a spider pattern wet fly designed to be fished on the spate rivers. This nymph pattern is an entirely different dressing for a different purpose – for the small stillwater trout fisheries of the South of England, where the leaded version is particularly useful. It is a highly visible nymph and has been known to attract a rainbow trout cruising some ten yards away. It is also good in coloured water.

DRESSING

Hook: Size 10 or 8 long-shank, lead optional.
Tying silk: Black.
Tail: White cock hackle-fibres.
Body: Orange floss ribbed with copper wire.
Thorax: Orange floss.
Wing-cases: White feather-fibres.
Hackle: Brown partridge.
Head: Black varnish.

1 Superla Bug   **2** Partridge and Orange   **3** Persuader   **4** Zugbug
5 Westward Bug   **6** Black Leech   **7** Woolly Worm   **8** Stick Fly

3 Persuader

COMMENT

One of John Goddard's many fine patterns, the Persuader was designed to give the impression of a sedge pupa, and it works well when fished on a floating line at sedge time. However, it has a double role, for it has also proved its worth as a fry imitator.

DRESSING

Hook: Size 10 or 8 long-shank, lead optional.
Tying silk: Black or orange.
Body: Five strands of white ostrich herl ribbed with oval silver tinsel.
Thorax: Orange seal's fur.
Wing-cases: Brown turkey tail feather.
Head: Black or orange varnish.

4 Zugbug

COMMENT

This is an American nymph which when leaded has proved a winner on our small stillwater fisheries. It can be used to represent a caddis, damsel-fly or dragon-fly larva as well as other bottom-dwellers. Trout take it well even when the water is very clear. At such times the fish have plenty of time to inspect it, so it must look realistic.

DRESSING

Hook: Size 10 or 8 long-shank with leaded underbody.
Tying silk: Black.
Tail: Bronze peacock herl.
Body: Bronze peacock herl ribbed with silver wire.
Hackle: Dark brown cock.
Wing: Silver mallard cut to leave ½-inch of stubble end.
Head: Black varnish.

5 Westward Bug

COMMENT

I designed this leaded nymph especially for small fisheries such as Avington. At its first outing there the nymph brought me my best-ever rainbow, a fish of 16¾lb that had refused plenty of anglers' flies that day before taking mine. Six weeks later I had another day at Avington to do some filming for Westward TV. Once again the nymph performed brilliantly, taking rainbow trout weighing 9lb and 8¾lb, plus brook trout of 3lb and 3lb 4½oz, the latter a new English record. I named the nymph in remembrance of the day.

DRESSING

Hook: Size 8 long-shank bronze.
Tying silk: Brown.
Underbody: Lead the underside of the hook-shank with strip lead. Tie in a spray of pheasant feather-fibres as a shellback.
Body: Several strands of dark brown marabou herl ribbed with orange floss.
Hackle: Honey-coloured hackle-fibres. Throat only.
Back: Pull down tight the pheasant fibres already tied in and secure them at the head.
Head: Clear varnish to give a brown finish.

6 Black Leech

COMMENT

The simple tying of the Black Leech should not detract from its importance as an excellent trout-catcher. It really does work well when fished early in the season, from March through to May. Use it singly on a long leader and a floating or sinking line according to the depth of water.

DRESSING

Hook: Size 10 or 8 long-shank with leaded underbody.
Tying silk: Black.
Tail: Long black hackle-fibres or marabou.
Body: Black suede chenille.
Shellback head: Black feather-fibre.
Hackle: Black hen.
Head: Black varnish.

7 Woolly Worm

COMMENT

The Woolly Worm is known to the Americans as a catcher of big fish – 'lunkers', as they call them. It is also a favourite of Alan Pearson, well-known for the big rainbows he has caught. He regularly discarded better-known top droppers in favour of the 'Worm'. I was with him when he caught a fine wild brown trout of nearly 3lb on it from Lough Mask. Later it caught him the best brown trout in the annual Pro-Am competition at Rutland. The fish weighed 3½lb.

DRESSING

Hook: Size 10 or 8 long-shank.
Tying silk: Black.
Tail: Red feather-fibre.
Body: Brown floss or wool ribbed with gold tinsel.
Body hackle: Ginger brown cock thickly palmered.
Head: Black varnish.

8 Stick Fly

COMMENT

Sedge hatches are important on most trout waters, but before they occur the larva form of the fly is creeping about the bottom. Trout feed on the larvae, or caddis grubs, one of which provides a sizeable meal. The larvae build tubular protective cases of whatever materials are available, but the trout eat them whole. The Stick Fly imitates one of these cases. Fish the fly slow and deep on a floating or sink-tip fly-line and a long leader.

DRESSING

Hook: Size 6, 8 or 10 long-shank bronze.
Tying silk: Black.
Body: Four strands of bronze peacock herl reinforced with an anticlockwise rib of copper wire.
Thorax: Yellow or amber wool or seal's fur.
Hackle: Two full turns of long-fibred honey, ginger or brown hen hackle.
Head: Black varnish.

Dry Flies

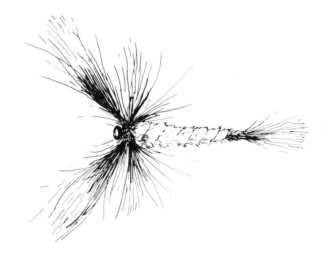

Introduction to Dry Flies

There are many types of dry fly, from the heavily-hackled Bi-visible sedges to the size 16 Olive Smuts. There are Spent Mayflies and Fan-winged Mayflies, and even cork-bodied Daddy-long-legs and buoyant Ethafoam Dead-fish floating lures. What would the chalk-stream masters of yesteryear have said about those, I wonder?

Dry-fly fishing used to be described as a waste of time on stillwaters, but much has now been learned about the effectiveness of dry patterns on reservoirs and lakes. In July and August a single dry Sedge fished static can provide the best method of taking a fish on a flat-calm evening. I have seen it work time and time again. A good, well-oiled pattern, confidence and patience are all that are needed. Sooner or later a fish will find the fly and take.

Earlier in the year, during May, the first of the upright-winged lake olives begin to appear. Wet flies or nymphs work well by day, but a dry fly scores best in the evening. Later in the summer, the drone fly or hoverfly may suddenly appear in millions during a prolonged hot spell. When they do, the angler who is ready for them with the appropriate fly will be the one who catches. The flying ant often appears in great swarms under the same conditions, falling spent on the water's surface. Again, it pays to have a decent artificial ready in your box.

Some waters – my own home water, Pitsford, is one – are plagued by tremendous hatches of Caenis, that tiny fly known as the 'anglers' curse'. Trout often become completely preoccupied when this happens and are difficult to tempt. However, those well-known river dry-fly patterns, Grey Duster and Tup's Indispensable, often catch fish when all else fails. Towards the back-end of the season, in late August and September, nothing is so effective as the Daddy-long-legs or Crane-fly.

Most of the flies included in this book are intended for the stillwater fly-fisher. However, I have included my favourite river patterns as well. I have spent some super days dry-fly fishing on the Test, Kennet and Itchen, the Derbyshire Wye, the Lathkill and the Manifold among others, but time prevents my doing as much river trout fishing as I would like. Some of my favourite river patterns are Spent Mayfly, Blue-winged Olive, Pheasant Tail, Coachman (Parachute-hackled), Iron Blue Dun, Sherry Spinner, Black Gnat, Kite's Imperial, Greenwell's Glory and the Grey Duster. It's the last of these that I've chosen for my sample tying.

I suggest a size 14 or size 16 for the hook. It may be up-eyed or down-eyed, as you prefer, but do select a fine-wire pattern. Having fixed it in the vice, wind a length of fine, pre-waxed brown tying silk down to just before the bend and catch-in a few fairly long fibres of a well-marked badger hackle as the tail. They should be about half as long again as the length of the hook-shank. For the body you need the blue underbody fur from a wild rabbit – make sure you do have only the underbody, and that no guard hairs are included to spoil the overall effect. The fur should be dubbed on to the tying silk in the usual way and then wound to form a neat carrot-shaped body, with at least 1mm of space left between the eye and the body to give room for the hackle to be wound on.

The choice of hackle is important. You need a well-marked badger hackle and the length of the fibres should be about twice the hook-gape. Catch-in the hackle over the bare silk behind the eye of the hook and wind on four or five turns. Tie in the point and trim off the excess stalk and tip. Build up a small, neat head, whip-finish and apply a couple of coats of Vycoat. What could be simpler? Even if you've never tied dry fly before, you now have a good fish-atcher to put in your box.

Incidentally, one of the latest items of ackle for the dry-fly fisher is a floating ersion of the sink-tip hollow-braided butt xtension leaders such as I mentioned for ymph-fishing. They are of the same length s the sink-tip version – 2 metres – but taper to the very finest tip. They are widely used by dry-fly fishers on the Continent. I first tried them at the Game Fair with Barrie Welham, and we were both impressed with the excellent turn-over of the fly, which gave great accuracy. They are now available throughout the world.

Dry Flies 1

This is a selection of the larger dry flies. Most are suitable for stillwater fishing and are often best fished static. Each has its seasonal role to play. Perhaps the best-known, even to non-fishers, is the Daddy-long-legs. Then there's the Mayfly, and with the natural seeming to appear everywhere these days it's a good idea to hav a few tyings in your box. Dave Tait's fly-line representation of the spent fly is particularly good. Another winner is John Goddard and Cl Henry's G and H Sedge – a fabulous wake fly o the reservoirs.

1 Daddy-long-legs

COMMENT

The crane-fly, or Daddy-long-legs, is the most important fly as autumn approaches. It falls on to the surface of all our large lakes, pits and reservoirs, and on damp, muggy days you will see hundreds of these flies being blown on to the water. Trout love them, and if anything can move the big, sulky old specimens which live virtually all their life on the bottom, it's the Daddy. Fish the fly oiled to ensure that it floats well. I like to fish mine static or drifting with the wind.

DRESSING

Hook: Size 10 or 8 long-shank.
Tying silk: Black.
Body: Yellow floss ribbed with black tying silk.
Legs: Six pheasant-tail feather-fibres, each of them knotted.
Hackle: Blue-dun cock.
Wings: Two pairs of cree cock hackle-points.
Head: Black varnish.

2 Fly-line Fanwing Mayfly

COMMENT

Gloucestershire fly-tyer Dave Tait devised this excellent fly. It is the ultimate in non-sinking Mayflies and looks very realistic on the water's surface. Green or yellow fly-line may also be used, and the wing and hackle colours can be changed, too. I have fooled the wily Lough Mask brown trout with this fly, as well as Lechlade Trout Fishery's rainbow stockies.

DRESSING

Hook: Size 10 or 8 up-eyed.
Tying silk: Black.
Body (detached): White floating fly-line ribbed with black tying silk.
Tail (on detached body): Pheasant-tail feather-fibre.
Hackle: Brown cock.
Wings: Pair of mallard or duck breast feathers dyed pale yellow.
Head: Black varnish.

1 Daddy-long-legs **2** Fly-line Fanwing Mayfly **3** Brown Bi-visible
4 G and H Sedge **5** Red Wulff **6** Spent Mayfly **7** Irresistible
8 Black Bi-visible

3 Brown Bi-visible

COMMENT

As the name indicates, this thickly-hackled sedge is very visible. It is also very buoyant. It is an excellent pattern to be fished as a single static fly on stillwaters at sedge time, and it is amazing to see how well trout come up for it. Bi-visibles are of American origin.

DRESSING

Hook: Size 14, 12 or 10 up-eyed.
Tying silk: Brown or black.
Tail: Two brown cock hackle-tips.
Body: Two brown cock hackles, palmered tightly. If you begin at the hook-bend, you finish with the two tails ready-made.
Head hackle: Two full turns of white cock.
Head: Clear or black varnish.

4 G and H Sedge

COMMENT

John Goddard has contributed much to our understanding of underwater life and given us many hints in tying realistic artificials. The G and H sedge is the creation of John and his good friend, Cliff Henry. It has the perfect sedge silhouette shape when viewed from beneath – the trout's view. It can be fished as a static dry fly when green-bodied sedges are about, or skated across the top to make a V-wake.

DRESSING

Hook: Size 12 or 10 long-shank bronze.
Tying silk: Black or brown.
Tail and body: Thinly-spun natural deerhair trimmed to the shape of a resting sedge (with roof-shaped wings). A strand of waxed thread is secured at the hook-bend, and a little green seal's fur is dubbed on and pulled tight to form the underbelly.
Hackle: Two full, circular turns of light brown cock swept back.
Antennae: The two brown hackle-stalks.
Heads: Black or brown varnish.

5 Red Wulff

COMMENT

This is a good high-floating pattern from the famous American dry-fly series named after Lee Wulff, the professional fly-fisher and author. It offers a distinct spent silhouette to the fish.

DRESSING

Hook: Size 14, 12 or 10 up-eyed.
Tying silk: Black.
Tail: Natural bucktail.
Body: Red floss ribbed with silver oval thread.
Hackle: Brown cock.
Wings: Natural bucktail tied forward spent.
Head: Black varnish.

6 Spent Mayfly

I remember being caught out on a trip to Damerham, in Hampshire. Mayfly were hatching sparsely all day, and the occasional fish was rising to them. In the evening, when the females returned from the surrounding bushes where they had mated, they dipped on to the water and laid their eggs before lying spent on the surface. Suddenly the trout begin to rise, taking the spent fly in preference to all others. I quickly improvised the correct shape and took my limit.

Hook: Size 8 or 10 long-shank bronze.
Tying silk: Brown.
Tail: Four strands of pheasant-tail fibre.
Body: Thin white foam plastic or white floss ribbed with fine, oval tinsel.
Hackle: Four turns of long-fibred grizzle cock hackle, followed by two turns of shorter-fibred badger cock hackles.
Wing: Four cock hackles dyed violet-blue, two on each side, tied spent.
Head: Clear varnish.

7 Irresistible

I have had some good results with this virtually-unsinkable dry fly in competitions when small rainbows have been up and about in the waves. Normally I put it on the point and fish it through the waves fairly quickly, creating a small wake. It certainly catches a lot of stockies, much needed in competitions. The fly is of American origin.

Hook: Size 12 or 10 up-eyed.
Tying silk: Black.
Tail: Brown cock hackle-fibres.
Body: Clipped natural deerhair.
Hackle: Brown cock.
Wings: Grizzle cock hackle-tips.
Head: Black varnish.

8 Black Bi-visible

This is a good fly to be fished static. Try it on a size 14 in an early-season buzzer rise. You will be impressed at the results. Both Brown and Black Bi-visibles have a second use as top droppers for boat fishing on reservoirs or lochs.

Hook: Size 14, 12 or 10 up-eyed.
Tying silk: Black.
Tail: Two black cock hackle-tips.
Body: Two black cock hackles, palmered tightly. If you begin at the hook-bend, you will finish with the two tails ready-made.
Head hackle: Two full turns of white cock.
Head: Black varnish.

Dry Flies 2

This is a varied selection. The Rat's Tail is unusual with its buoyant deerhair body, but it works extremely well. The idea has been developed into a series with differently-coloured deerhair. Dyeing the various colours does entail a lot of work, but is a worthwhile operation. Cyril Inwood always preferred his own Ginger Palmer to the Soldier Palmer which has now become so popular. Another of Cyril's patterns was the Drone Fly, which caught him some excellent limit-bags at Grafham when others were going home fishless.

1 White Wulff

COMMENT

This is another dry fly from American angler Lee Wulff. It has excellent high-floating qualities and is good at mayfly time. The time to fish this pattern is when the female fly returns to lay her eggs and finally lies spent on the surface. The pattern is also good on big reservoirs that have intense Caenis hatches during the hot, still evenings of summer.

DRESSING

Hook: Size 14, 12 or 10 up-eyed.
Tying silk: Black.
Tail: White bucktail.
Body: White floss silk.
Hackle: Badger cock.
Wing: White bucktail tied spent forward.
Head: Black varnish.

2 Webb's Winged Palmer

COMMENT

This pattern was devised by Richard Webb, from Higham Ferrers. Richard is a very good top-of-the-water flyfisher at Grafham, but when most anglers are using the Soldier Palmer, he is using his own pattern and proving its worth with his results. Fish it in the waves on the top dropper and bob while drifting.

DRESSING

Hook: Size 14, 12 or 10.
Tying silk: Black.
Body: Blood-red (almost claret) seal's fur ribbed with silver oval tinsel.
Body hackle: Dark brown cock.
Wing: Brown feather-fibre.
Front hackle: Dark brown cock.
Head: Black varnish.

1 White Wulff **2** Webb's Winged Palmer **3** Wickham's Fancy **4** Yellow Hackle
5 Rat's Tail **6** Renegade **7** Inwood's Ginger Palmer **8** Drone Fly

3 Wickham's Fancy (dry)

COMMENT

The Wickham's is superb as a wet fly, and as a dry it is one of the best sedge imitations. Use it singly on a light cast for stillwater trout feeding selectively in crystal-clear water. Such conditions occur regularly at gravel-pit trout fisheries and at reservoirs after heavy rain. The best months for the Wickham's are July and August, when it is also of great value to the river angler.

DRESSING

Hook: Size 14, 12 or 10 up-eyed.
Tying silk: Black.
Tail: Ginger cock hackle-fibres.
Body: Gold Lurex.
Body Hackle: Ginger cock, palmered.
Wing: Grey starling tied upright.
Head: Black varnish.

4 Yellow Hackle

COMMENT

I have found the Yellow Hackle useful as a top or centre dropper in the main summer period from June to September. It can be used wet or dry. It is easy to tie and a good starter fly for someone new to fly-dressing.

DRESSING

Hook: Size 12 or 10.
Tying silk: Brown.
Tail: Crimson cock fibres.
Body: Yellow floss ribbed with grey floss.
Hackle: Long-fibred ginger-brown cock.
Head: Clear varnish.

5 Rat's Tail

COMMENT

This dry fly was the brainchild of Roy Parker. He and his friend, the experienced Hector Woolnough, are Pitsford regulars, and their favourite method of fishing both there and elsewhere is to boat fish on the drift, but with dry flies. After using all the accepted hackled dry flies, Roy decided he wanted one that was completely unsinkable. His idea of using buoyant deerhair in the body and tail of his Rat's Tail did the trick. The fly was developed into a series with varying colours of dyed deerhair. Olive, yellow and black are alternatives.

DRESSING

Hook: Size 14, 12 or 10 up- or down-eyed.
Tying silk: Black.
Tail and body: Brown deerhair ribbed with black tying silk.
Hackle: Brown cock or olive.
Head: Black varnish.

6 Renegade

COMMENT

The idea of the fore-and-aft hackle of this American pattern is to give maximum buoyancy and create surface disturbance as the fly is retrieved. Richard Walker found an unusual way of catching trout with this pattern. One day, while having a sandwich, Dick left his sinking line lying along the bottom, so that the fore-and-aft fly was also static on the bottom. Suddenly the reel screeched – Richard struck and hooked a trout. Other anglers tried the 'method', but with limited success. My verdict is that this method is too boring. Keep this fly for fishing the surface.

DRESSING

Hook: Size 14, 12 or 10 up-eyed.
Tying silk: Black.
Tag: Gold Lurex.
Rear hackle: Medium-brown cock.
Body: Bronze peacock herl.
Front hackle: White cock.
Head: Black varnish.

7 Inwood's Ginger Palmer

COMMENT

Although Cyril Inwood died several years ago, he is still remembered as an outstanding fly-fisher. He often used this variation of the Soldier Palmer dry fly when he was short-lining, loch-style, from a boat drifting in a big wave. He would put this bushy fly on the top dropper with a sober-coloured wet fly on the centre dropper and a flasher on the point. The Palmer bobbed in the waves and brought up the fish, even though they often took one of the other flies. His method still works just as well.

DRESSING

Hook: Size 14, 12 or 10 up-eyed bronze.
Tying silk: Black.
Body: Gold Lurex tinsel ribbed with fine gold wire.
Body hackle: Ginger-brown cock hackle tied fully circular.
Hackle: Ginger-brown cock hackle tied bushy.
Head: Black varnish.

8 Drone Fly

COMMENT

The first man to connect trout with these small wasp-like flies was Cyril Inwood. During the late 1960s this fly used to appear at Grafham during hot periods in late summer and Cyril tied some dry fly imitations of it. He immediately caught a lot of big rainbows which were completely preoccupied in feeding on the natural. Frank Cutler, Cyril's old friend, qualified in the 1985 English National, also on Grafham, with eight rainbows. This fly is a 'must' for hot days in late summer.

DRESSING

Hook: Size 14, 12 or 10 up-eyed.
Tying silk: Black.
Body: Yellow midge floss ribbed with a strand of bronze peacock herl.
Hackle: Ginger cock.
Wings: White or honey cock hackle-tips.
Head: Black varnish.

Dry Flies 3

Most of the flies in this selection are important river patterns, but they can also be used to good effect on stillwaters. Halford's Ginger Quill can be relied on to take fish in many otherwise uncertain situations, and so can the Lake Olive and the Black Gnat. The Flying Black Ant and the Cowdung also work well on the right occasion.

1 Royal Coachman

COMMENT

Originally a wet fly, the Royal Coachman is merely an overdressed American version of the English Coachman. It dates back to 1878 and was introduced by John Haily, a top angler of his day. Well thought of in Scotland, it is only in more recent years that the Royal Coachman has been used for dry-fly fishing.

DRESSING

Hook: Size 16, 14, 12 or 10 up-eyed.
Tying silk: Black.
Tail: Brown cock hackle-fibres.
Tag: Bronze peacock herl.
Body: Red floss ribbed with fine silver wire.
Thorax: Bronze peacock herl.
Hackle: Medium-brown cock.
Wing: White bucktail hair or white feather tied spent forward.
Head: Black varnish.

2 Cowdung

COMMENT

There is no need to enlarge on the habitat of the natural that this pattern represents. Cowdung flies are abundant during March and April and often find their way on to rivers and sometimes on to stillwaters, probably blown there by the wind. Even if only a few cowdung flies reach the river's surface, trout will still rise for them because fly-life is scarce in these early months and the fish are looking for food. This dry fly pattern can be used with confidence at such times.

DRESSING

Hook: Size 16, 14, 12 or 10 up-eyed.
Tying silk: Black.
Body: Pale olive floss.
Hackle: Brown cock.
Wings: Medium-brown feather-fibre tied upright.
Head: Black varnish.

1 Royal Coachman **2** Cowdung **3** The White Moth **4** Halford's Ginger Quill
5 Quill Gordon **6** Flying Black Ant **7** Black Gnat **8** Lake Olive

3 The White Moth

COMMENT

The White Moth imitates the ghost and swift moths, which are reasonably common throughout Britain. Fish it on a floating line and partially-greased leader and cast so as to drop the fly with a 'plop'. This simulates the natural moth, which does fall rather heavily on to the water. This pattern has accounted for some very good trout – and some specimen carp! It is obviously a pattern with which to experiment as well as to fish at the appropriate time.

DRESSING

Hook: Size 14, 12 or 10 medium-shank bronze.
Tail: Golden-pheasant tippets.
Body: White ostrich herl.
Hackle: Four turns of white cock.
Wing: White swan or goose.
Head: Black varnish.

4 Halford's Ginger Quill

COMMENT

This is a 'must' for any river fly-fisher, whether he be on the Barle or the Itchen, the Usk or the Driffield Beck. The fly is best used when pale wateries or light olives are coming off. It is a good dry fly for the early months of the year, although an all-hackled version can be used with good results later on during sedge time.

DRESSING

Hook: Size 16, 14, 12 or 10 up-eyed.
Tying silk: Black.
Tail: Pale ginger cock hackle-fibres.
Body: Stripped peacock quill dyed brown.
Hackle: Pale ginger cock.
Wings: Pale grey starling tied upright.
Head: Black varnish.

5 Quill Gordon

COMMENT

Invented by a famous American dry-fly fisherman, Theodore Gordon, in the nineteenth century, the Quill Gordon was voted the number one dry fly by a group of influential anglers from New York some years ago. It has travelled well and is a good general river pattern. It works particularly well at the beginning of mayfly time.

DRESSING

Hook: Size 16, 14, 12 or 10 up-eyed.
Tying silk: Black.
Tail: Blue-dun cock hackle-fibres.
Body: Pale grey stripped quill.
Hackle: Blue-dun cock.
Wings: Duck or mallard breast feather dyed pale yellow and tied upright.
Head: Black varnish.

6 Flying Black Ant

COMMENT

Occasionally on a reservoir on a baking hot day, when not much is doing, large numbers of flying black ants suddenly drop on to the water. This invariably results in an instant rise, even though conditions are bright and flat calm. I remember one such day at Ravensthorpe when sport was first-class once I put on the right dry fly. It pays to have a good artificial at 'ant time' as the fish do become rather selective – and this is a good one.

DRESSING

Hook: Size 14, 12 or 10 up-eyed.
Tying silk: Black.
Body: Black floss, shaped and varnished.
Hackle: Black cock.
Wings: White hackle-tips tied upright.
Head: Black varnish.

7 Black Gnat

COMMENT

This dry Black Gnat pattern covers just about any black fly which is liable to appear on the surface of any British stillwater. Early-season black chironomids, the Hawthorn fly, dark sedges – you name it and this one will fit the bill. As well as being a good stillwater fly, the Black Gnat is a reliable standby on most northern and Welsh rivers, and it demonstrates occasional flashes of brilliance on chalkstreams, too.

DRESSING

Hook: Size 16, 14, 12 or 10 up-eyed.
Tying silk: Black.
Tail: Black cock hackle-fibres.
Body: Black floss silk.
Hackle: Black cock.
Wing: Light grey starling tied upright.
Head: Black varnish.

8 Lake Olive

COMMENT

I fish this pattern with confidence when the olives begin to hatch, which is usually around the third week in May. It is then a very good dry fly to fish singly off the bank. One of the most pleasing sights I know as a fly-fisher is that of scores of olives drifting downwind or downstream like miniature sailing-boats. You can be sure that at this time there will be some exciting sport.

DRESSING

Hook: Size 16, 14, 12 or 10 up-eyed.
Tying silk: Black.
Tail: Dark olive hackle-fibres.
Body: Dark olive seal's fur ribbed with fine silver oval tinsel.
Hackle: Dark olive cock.
Wing: Dark grey starling tied upright.
Head: Black varnish.

Dry Flies 4

Some classic river patterns are included in this selection. Even Skues would have approved of them, though I fancy he would have had reservations about some of those described elsewhere in the book. I would never fish a river without having a Greenwell's, an Iron Blue and a Kite's Imperial to hand; and the Grey Duster and the Tup's work well on reservoirs during a sedge hatch. But the real message is for the chalk-stream man: They're all 'musts'.

1 Kite's Imperial

COMMENT

Oliver Kite was a most respected fly-fisher, entomologist and journalist, and he will always be remembered for this fine dry fly. He created the Imperial after a day's fishing on the Teifi, in Wales, early in the 1962 season. That day Oliver carefully studied specimens of the male large olive dun, and the new dry fly was born. It has proved a winner for river-fishers ever since.

DRESSING

Hook: Size 16, 14 or 12 up-eyed.
Tying silk: Black.
Tail: Brown cock hackle-fibres.
Body: Heron herl ribbed with fine gold wire.
Thorax: Heron herl.
Hackle: Light ginger or honey cock.
Head: Black varnish.

2 Tup's Indispensable

COMMENT

Devised by R.S. Austin about 1900, the Tup's has become a popular fly, fished either wet or dry. I often use it when the trout are on Caenis (the anglers' curse). It usually takes a few fish at this difficult time. I fish it in sizes 14 or 16, either as a static dry fly or retrieved an inch at a time on a leader of 2½–3lb nylon.

DRESSING

Hook: Size 14, 16 or 18 bronze up-eyed.
Tying silk: Black.
Tail: Blue-dun whisks.
Body: Primrose floss for two-thirds of hook-shank.
Thorax: Pinky-red dubbed seal's fur.
Hackle: Three full turns of blue-dun cock.
Head: Black.

1 Kite's Imperial   **2** Tup's Indispensable   **3** Houghton Ruby   **4** Sherry Spinner
5 Greenwell's Glory   **6** Coachman Dry   **7** Grey Duster   **8** Iron Blue Dun

3 Houghton Ruby

COMMENT

It was the famous river-keeper of the Houghton Club, W.J. Lunn, who gave us this successful pattern. It is intended to imitate the iron blue female spinner, which it does better than most other artificials. It is a favourite dry fly of most knowledgeable chalk-stream fishers.

DRESSING

Hook: Size 16, 14 or 12 up-eyed.
Tying silk: Black.
Tail: Three fibres of white cock hackle.
Body: Red quill or red floss.
Hackle: Dark brown.
Wing: Two honey-white cock hackle-tips (sometimes tied spent) clipped at the points.
Head: Black varnish.

4 Sherry Spinner

COMMENT

This dry fly represents the female spinner of the blue-winged olive, a common fly on many rivers and streams in June and July. The spinners drop on to the water towards dark, and it is then that this artificial is best used.

DRESSING

Hook: Size 16, 14 or 12 up-eyed.
Tying silk: Black.
Tail: Honey cock hackle-fibres.
Body: Well mix orange, yellow and a little green seal's fur (or substitute) with a touch of hare's fur. Prepare enough for several flies. It is dubbed on and ribbed with fine gold wire.
Hackle: Pale honey cock.
Wing: Very fine honey cock hackle-tips.
Head: Black varnish.

5 Greenwell's Glory

COMMENT

The Greenwell's is perhaps the best of the dual-purpose wet or dry flies. It is particularly effective on stillwaters when fish are 'on' olives and buzzers and on the rivers it is regarded as possibly the best of the general patterns. It was first used during the last century by Canon Greenwell, of Durham. Incidentally, to me coch-y-bondhu hackles are the black-centred feathers with dark brown tips.

DRESSING

Hook: Size 16, 14 or 12 up-eyed.
Tying silk: Black or yellow.
Body: Yellow tying silk or floss, ribbed with fine gold wire.
Hackle: Greenwell's cock (pale honey-coloured tip with a black centre). The old books called it the coch-y-bondhu.
Wing: The original was blackbird, but dark starling is perfect.
Head: Clear or black varnish.

6 Coachman Dry

COMMENT

John Neville gave me a Parachute-hackled Coachman to put on as we started fishing one day for the wild rainbows of the Derbyshire Wye. I caught 23 fish on it before lunch. It finished up tattered and torn, but that fly really did the trick. To tie it, simply substitute a white Parachute hackle for the normal wing in the dressing given. By the way, as in most river fishing these days we kept only a brace apiece. The origin of the Coachman is said to lie with Mr Tom Basworth, a coachman to George IV, William IV and Queen Victoria.

DRESSING

Hook: Size 16, 14 or 12 up-eyed.
Tying silk: Black.
Body: Bronze peacock herl.
Hackle: Dark brown cock.
Wings: White duck or swan.
Head: Black varnish.

7 Grey Duster

COMMENT

The Grey Duster, a great dry fly on both stillwaters and rivers, has its roots in Wales, where it is much praised. My experience of this fly on the reservoirs has shown it to be one of the few patterns which can bring sport during hatches of the dreaded Caenis (anglers' curse). It is the first fly I put on whenever I fish a rough, shallow mountain stream. It is excellent in such conditions.

DRESSING

Hook: Size 16, 14 or 12 up-eyed.
Tying silk: Black or brown.
Body: Dubbed light rabbit fur.
Hackle: Well-marked badger cock.
Head: Black or clear varnish.

8 Iron Blue Dun

COMMENT

Trout are particularly partial to the natural iron blue dun, even though it is so small. If three different flies are hatching at once, and one is the iron blue, you will almost certainly find that the rising trout are taking only the iron blue. Harry Plunket-Greene wrote in *Where the Bright Waters Meet*, 'If I was to be limited to one dry fly only for the rest of my life, I would stick with the Iron Blue Quill.' It is a 'must' for all river-fishers, nationwide.

DRESSING

Hook: Size 16 or 14 up-eyed.
Tying silk: Black or red.
Tail: Pale grey-blue cock.
Body: Quill dyed ink-blue. Fine gold wire ribbing is optional.
Hackle: Dark blue-dun cock.
Wings: Starling dyed ink-blue.
Head: Black or clear varnish.

Dry Flies 5

This selection is a mixture of river and lake patterns, but mostly river, with the Pale Watery, Blue-winged Olive, Pheasant Tail and Lunn's Caperer high in many fly-fishers' esteem. The odd one out is possibly The Priest, because it was originally intended as a grayling fly.

However, it now has a new lease of life as a successful stillwater trout pattern. If you tie up a few of each of the five sets of dry flies I have described, you will have enough patterns for almost all river fishing in Great Britain and Ireland.

1 Pale Watery Dun

COMMENT

One of the smaller members of the ephemeroptera, the pale watery hatches begin in May and continue throughout the season. The fly is common on most British rivers, and when two or three types of fly are hatching together, it is often the small pale watery dun that the trout prefer. You can fish this dry fly with confidence.

DRESSING

Hook: Size 16, 14 or 12 up-eyed.
Tying silk: Black.
Tail: Blue-dun cock hackle-fibres.
Body: Light grey seal's fur or Antron.
Hackle: Blue-dun cock.
Wings: Light starling.
Head: Black varnish.

2 Blue-winged Olive

COMMENT

The blue-winged olive is one of the commonest of the delicate upwinged flies found on most rivers in the British Isles. A number of schools of thought exist about its tying, but the dressing given is, in my opinion, as good as any. One elderly Hampshire chalk-stream fisherman always impressed on me that size of fly is as important as the dressing. Certainly I have known numerous occasions when I could catch fish after fish on a size 14 Blue-winged Olive yet could take hardly one on a size 16 or a size 12.

DRESSING

Hook: Size 16, 14 or 12 up-eyed.
Tying silk: Black.
Tail: Light olive cock hackle-fibres.
Body: Grey-green condor herl ribbed with fine gold wire.
Hackle: Light olive cock.
Wings: Light grey starling.
Head: Black varnish.

1 Pale Watery Dun **2** Blue-winged Olive **3** The Priest **4** Mosquito Midge
5 Olive Smut **6** Treacle Parkin **7** Pheasant Tail **8** Lunn's Caperer

3 The Priest

COMMENT

In its original form The Priest was used mostly for grayling and always as a wet fly. However, in recent years it has become known as a dry fly. It works well in a Caenis hatch and can sometimes be very good in a buzzer hatch. It is really of unknown potential. Try it for yourself.

DRESSING

Hook: Size 16, 14 or 12 up-eyed.
Tying silk: Black.
Tail: Red ibis.
Body: Silver Lurex ribbed with silver wire.
Hackle: Badger cock.
Head: Black varnish.

4 Mosquito Midge

COMMENT

I am not sure how this dry-fly pattern came into my possession; it must have been given to me by a fellow-angler some time in the distant past. However, one day at Draycote I put it on after a series of fruitless fly-changes and quickly caught seven fish to complete a limit. Before that hour's burst of activity, I had fished for five hours for one fish. It works well when the early small, dark chironomids are 'on'.

DRESSING

Hook: Size 16, 14 or 12 up-eyed.
Tying silk: Brown or olive.
Tail: White hackle-fibres.
Body: Brown tying silk ribbed with black tying silk.
Hackle: Grizzle cock.
Wing: A pair of grizzle cock hackle-tips.
Head: Clear varnish.

5 Olive Smut

COMMENT

This tiny dry fly is to be called upon only in desperation. Sometimes in a flat calm millions of tiny smuts hover above a lake's surface and then drop spent on to the water. On many occasions I have seen trout swimming slowly and sedately along completely preoccupied with sucking in these minute flies. This is the time to try an Olive Smut on a 2lb point. The fly once worked for me from the bank at Rutland and caught a near-3lb rainbow in seemingly impossible conditions. A few eyebrows were raised that hot, sunny afternoon!

DRESSING

Hook: Size 18 or 16 up-eyed.
Tying silk: Olive.
Tail: Honey cock hackle-fibres.
Body: Light olive floss.
Hackle: Light olive cock.
Wings: A pair of honey cock hackle-tips.
Head: Clear varnish.

6 Treacle Parkin

COMMENT

The Treacle Parkin looks rather like a Coch-y-bondhu with a yellow tail. Those well-known Yorkshire anglers, Tim Wilson and Charles Derrick always rated this pattern highly on their home rivers. The Treacle Parkin is also similar to the Red Tag, though the latter has a red tail. It is a good general-purpose dry fly.

DRESSING

Hook: Size 16, 14 or 12 up-eyed.
Tying silk: Black.
Tail: Bunched yellow floss silk.
Body: Bronze peacock herl wound quite bulkily.
Hackle: Dark brown coch-y-bondhu.
Head: Black varnish.

7 Pheasant Tail

COMMENT

Invented by Payne Collier just after the turn of the century for the rough rivers and streams of Devon, this dry fly has become famous the world over. I always try it on a river when little is hatching, and it has scored for me on the Test when Iron Blues have been coming off. I once enticed an old 'uncatchable' big fish to take on it after I had been told the fish was so educated that he would die of old age. He probably did, too, because he broke my 2lb point.

DRESSING

Hook: Size 16, 14, 12 up-eyed.
Tying silk: Black or brown.
Tail: Honey cock hackle-fibres or pheasant-tail fibres.
Body: Pheasant-tail feather-fibres ribbed with gold wire.
Hackle: Medium-brown cock or blue-dun cock.
Head: Black or clear varnish.

8 Lunn's Caperer

COMMENT

The caperer is yet another sedge, but of a light cinnamon colour. It hatches on many rivers during August and September. Lunn's artificial is as good as any. A mystery from times gone by is why Halford insisted on calling it the Welshman's Button when that, in fact, is a beetle.

DRESSING

Hook: Size 16, 14 or 12 up-eyed.
Tying silk: Black.
Body: Brown condor herl with a ring of yellow condor herl in the centre.
Hackle: Medium-brown cock.
Head: Black varnish.

Bob Church's Personal Favourites

You can take it from me that all the flies in this set are very good indeed. They are all favourites of mine which are little-known and rarely mentioned in the fishing press. Old Nick has proved deadly in hot midsummer weather, beating all others as a top dropper for rainbows.

Another fine top dropper is the Thicket, while Fat Boy is a great point-fly. The Ardleigh Nymph, devised at Ardleigh by Richard Connell, is a superb deceiver pattern and will tempt any nymphing trout. Yes, this really is a great selection.

1 Munro Killer

COMMENT

The Munro is really a most effective salmon fly, but it occurred to me that it might work well for rainbows, like that other famous Scottish fly, the Dunkeld. Sure enough, trial fishing showed that it worked just as well. It is well worth tying one or two to be used as change point-flies for loch-style boat fishing with a floating line.

DRESSING

Hook: Size 12, 10 or 8 medium-shank.
Tying silk: Black.
Tag: Gold Lurex.
Tail: Orange hackle-tips.
Body: Black floss ribbed with oval gold.
Body hackle: Orange cock, palmered.
Hackle: Blue jay; throat only.
Wing: Grey squirrel dyed yellow and showing a black bar.
Head: Black varnish.

2 Ardleigh Nymph

COMMENT

This nymph was devised by Ardleigh Reservoir fishery manager, Richard Connell, and he has tremendous faith in it as a general nymph pattern. Fished during the evening, it is deadly in tempting brown trout during a rise to buzzer or sedge. The nymph was originally designed to imitate the emerging insect at Ardleigh, but I have tried it on several other reservoirs with good results.

DRESSING

Hook: Size 16, 14, 12 or 10.
Tying silk: Black.
Tail: Greenwell's hackle-fibres.
Body: Pheasant-tail fibres ribbed with gold thread.
Thorax: Peacock herl.
Hackle: Small Greenwell's hen.
Head: Black varnish.

1 Munro Killer **2** Ardleigh Nymph **3** Thicket **4** Grousewing Sedge
5 Fat Boy **6** Old Nick **7** Suede Sedge **8** Silverhorn Sedge

3 Thicket

COMMENT

Used as a top dropper bob-fly, the Thicket will deceive trout in a high wave or at dusk. It can be used to represent almost anything, from a sedge to a terrestrial insect blown on to the water. I have tried it purely as a dry fly, fishing it singly and static – a tactic that works well in flat calm or light breeze.

DRESSING

Hook: Size 12 or 10 medium-shank.
Tying silk: Black.
Body: Gold Bobbydazzlelure.
Body hackles: Two olive grizzle cock tied palmer-style.
Wing (optional): Hen pheasant.
Head: Black varnish.

4 Grousewing Sedge

COMMENT

That experienced fly-fisher, Frank Cutler, once said to me: 'Even though thousands of these grousewing sedges are hatching, I don't think the trout like them very much. They prefer the silverhorn.' His theory was that grousewings were bitter to the taste, having tried one which flew into his mouth! However, this particular artificial Grousewing does work. It deceives trout very well when fished slowly across the surface on a floating line. The upwind bank at evening is the best place and time to use it, with July and August the best months.

DRESSING

Hook: Size 12 or 10 up-eyed.
Tying silk: Black.
Body: Gold Lurex ribbed with gold oval thread.
Body hackle: Ginger cock, palmered.
Wing: Pheasant rump feather.
Front hackle: Ginger cock.
Head: Black varnish.

5 Fat Boy

COMMENT

The Fat Boy's name comes from its fatter-than-normal body. It has produced some dramatic results when fished on a floating line, loch-style, at Rutland. A friend from New Zealand, trying Rutland for the first time, took browns of more than 4lb each for his first four fish. It has featured, too, as a competition-winning fly for anglers on both Rutland and Grafham.

DRESSING

Hook: Size 12, 10 or 8 medium-shank.
Tying silk: Black.
Tail: Brown bucktail.
Body: Claret Superla dubbing or seal's fur ribbed with silver oval thread.
Hackle: Brown hen.
Wing: Natural brown bucktail.
Head: Black varnish.

6 Old Nick

COMMENT

Introduced by Nick Nicholson, this attractor wet fly has been a killer of rainbow trout during high summer on the reservoirs. Hot-orange always seems to work when temperatures soar. I like to fish Old Nick on the top dropper and move it quite quickly through the waves.

DRESSING

Hook: Size 12 or 10 medium-shank.
Tying silk: Black.
Tail: Orange hackle-fibres.
Body: Gold Bobbydazzlelure.
Body hackle: Hot-orange cock, palmered.
Front hackle: Hot-orange cock.
Head: Black varnish.

7 Suede Sedge

COMMENT

Suede chenille is a much finer, more delicate chenille than other types and is ideal for small wet flies and nymphs. This realistic sedge pattern imitates the emerging pupa, a key stage in the sedge's life-cycle as far as the trout are concerned. Fish the fly very slowly in June and August. Evening is the best time, and use a floating line with a greased leader.

DRESSING

Hook: Size 12, 10 or 8.
Tying silk: Brown.
Body: Amber suede chenille ribbed with gold wire.
Thorax: Brown Superla dubbing or seal's fur.
Antennae: Bronze mallard feather-fibres.
Head: Clear varnish.

8 Silverhorn Sedge

COMMENT

The two most common sedge flies on rich lowland reservoirs and gravel-pits of central England are the silverhorn and the grousewing. This Silverhorn pattern was my 'find' of 1985. It is virtually a perfect imitation and will definitely be a principal fly for me at sedge time in the foreseeable future. It worked in all positions on the cast, but the point is probably best. Loch-style daytime fishing and upwind evening fishing from July through to September see the fly at its best.

DRESSING

Hook: Size 14, 12 or 10 medium-shank.
Tying silk: Black.
Body: Cream/buff seal's fur or Superla dubbing ribbed with fine silver oval thread.
Body hackle: Honey cock palmered.
Wing: Light brown feather-fibre.
Front hackle: Honey cock.
Antennae: Two pheasant-tail fibres.
Head: Black varnish.

Index